COMPETENCIES
IN ACTION

Jane Weightman B , MSc, PhD is a psycho…ist) has been associated with the Manchester School of Management at UMIST since
joining in 1980. She has carried out research into a wide range of management related topics. Previously she worked in the field of mental
handicap as a researcher, teacher, lecturer and county advisor. She has
written widely in a range of journals, and her books on management
include *Managing Human Resources* (2nd edition, 1993), (co-authored
with Derek Torrington) *Action Management: The essentials* (1991),
Managing People in the Health Service (1996), and *Managing People*
(1999), all published by the IPD.

COMPETENCIES
IN ACTION

Jane Weightman

INSTITUTE OF PERSONNEL AND DEVELOPMENT

First published in 1994
Reprinted 1995, 1998, 1999

Typesetting by The Comp-Room, Aylesbury
Printed in Great Britain by
The Cromwell Press, Trowbridge, Wiltshire

British Library Cataloguing-in-Publication Data
A catalogue record for this book is available from the
British Library

ISBN 0-85292-557-3

INSTITUTE OF PERSONNEL
AND DEVELOPMENT

IPD House, Camp Road, London SW19 4UX
Tel: 020 8971 9000   Fax: 020 8263 3333
Registered office as above. Registered Charity No. 1038333
A company limited by guarantee. Registered in England No. 2931892

Contents

Acknowledgements

I have tried to trace all owners of copyright material and am most grateful to those kind enough to grant me permission to reproduce it here: Bente Lowendahl of the Norwegian School of Management, for Figure 3.1; and the Institution of Civil Engineers, for Figures 5.2, 5.3, 5.4 and 5.5, which are taken from *Management Development in the Construction Industry* (Thomas Telford, 1992).

I would like to thank the people who asked to remain anonymous but generously gave me papers or told me about their competency schemes. I would also like to thank Matthew Reisz and the team at IPD for all their help.

1

Why Do I Need to Read a Book about Competency?

A personnel team leader in a large company which had introduced a competencies approach, whom I interviewed while researching this book, said:

> 'The framework is good. It is superb for developing staff, development planning and for promotions. I see enthusiasm, target setting and development plans. It plays up the behavioural side as well as the technical side. There is a balance between looking at behaviours, skills and knowledge. By involving folk we get the commitment.'

The team leader was talking about a home-grown scheme which had developed over several years, with local variations for each department based on a general format. The emphasis was on individual staff development.

There are other reasons for getting involved with competencies. There may be a top management initiative to look at 'core competencies' as the basis for strategic planning. There may be a desire for more systematic Human Resource Management. It may be a simpler reason, such as wanting to improve recruitment procedures or training. Yet another reason may be an initiative to try to ensure fairness and equality of employment and competencies are seen as a way of achieving this. For others, the reason for getting involved with competencies is that they keep hearing the word all over the place and there is so much discussion about competencies locally they feel it is time to be better informed. Some or all of these reasons may be why you need to read a book about competency, or you may have another reason altogether.

What is competency?

So what are competencies? (Much ink has been spilt on the precise distinction between competence/competences and competency/competencies; to simplify matters, I have used the latter terms throughout this text.) Essentially competencies underlie the behaviours thought necessary to achieve a desired outcome. A competency is something you can *demonstrate* – for example, 'change gear while driving a car' or 'slice bread' – where it is clear when the behaviour is successful. These in turn can be broken down into smaller steps, when the overall competency is difficult to achieve. Not all necessary work behaviours are easy to describe and analyse. Many of the most useful behaviours involve subtle application and experience to be effective, so where general statements of competency are wanted and these reflect higher order attributes, competency lists also include knowledge, understanding and personal attributes to temper the strictly behavioural descriptions of simpler competencies. For example, the Management Charter Initiative (MCI) managerial competency lists include sections on associated knowledge and understanding for each level. Further discussion of what competencies are can be found in Chapter 2.

So are competencies new? There is a long tradition of competency-based learning in areas such as engineering and science; just think of all those practical sessions! This competency-based learning has been directed mostly to acquiring technical competency at the bench, on the computer or on other equipment. However, increasingly there has been an interest in developing non-technical competencies, including among engineers and scientists. This has particularly focused on the interpersonal competencies of working with and influencing others, including such areas as project and team working, making presentations, dealing with customers, and contributing effectively in meetings, plus the non-technical aspects of work such as costing projects and using the administrative procedures.

So how do I use these competencies? A list of competencies appropriate for a particular job, profession or qualification can be drawn up by analysing and describing the behaviours and associated activities necessary to do specific aspects of the job. To this list is added the other behaviours that are likely to be required in the foreseeable future. Once we have drafted the list, an appropriate assessment procedure needs to be devised. Individuals can then be assessed against the list for selection, qualification or training and development purposes.

Aims of this book

The aim has been to help you to ask the right questions, rather than attempting to give 'right answers', if you are thinking of using a competency approach. The book is more about *what* to do than *how* to do it. This is because the right answers can only be found by ensuring that what you do really suits your particular needs and is not imposed, from someone else's perspective. I also believe that the process of working out what you want starts the process of implementing it, by getting people's commitment to try and make work the thing they have been involved in designing.

You are also encouraged to keep things as simple as possible. In the end, competencies should be used to *enhance* the main activity of your organisation not to become it. But this needs a caveat: avoid describing the obvious as that can lead to unworkable quantities. The clever thing is to identify the competencies which are critical but not obvious and routine. For example, we really do not need to list 'appropriate appearance' for sales staff but we probably do need to analyse and list 'customer focus' in some way.

The chapters are organised so you can use the book in different ways. Each chapter discusses the particular question given in the title of the chapter. These can be read in sequential order from Chapter 2 in the usual way. Alternatively, the chapters can be used separately, in any order, to tackle particular issues. Chapters 6, 7 and 8 are the most practical chapters, with an emphasis on how to do things, and have lots of detailed examples.

Each chapter includes descriptions of different ways of doing things, with some of the associated advantages and disadvantages. Which method, or combinations of methods, you choose is really up to you and what you set out to do. Within each chapter I have tried to give examples of current practice in organisations. These are not necessarily perfect as they are real examples but they can be helpful, if only to give you something to disagree with when trying to get going. There are also 'Questions to ask yourself' sections in the chapters which are intended to assist you in starting to think about your particular situation. There is no right answer to these questions, but you do need to think about them to make your use of competencies more competent. I

3

have included some references in the chapters if you want to read further but, as this is not intended as an academic book, I have kept these to a minimum.

My ambitions are for this to be a practical book for people working in organisations who want to introduce or develop the use of a competencies approach. It is aimed particularly at those who want to create their own lists to use and develop within their organisation, although often drawing on the advice and experience of others. By way of example of what is involved, the remainder of this chapter is devoted to two case studies of the development of home-grown lists of competencies.

A straightforward case of competency

We were involved in a straightforward project to use a competency approach with the personnel departments throughout a regional health authority. We, Derek Torrington, Will Blandamer and myself, were approached by the Regional Health Authority in 1990 to draw up a list of personnel competencies for personnel people throughout the region. We interviewed many of these people, at different levels in the hierarchy and in different districts; there were no trusts at this stage. We also looked at the current literature on personnel and were already very familiar with this particular profession.

To give bit of background to the case, under the changes imposed on health authorities by the Government at the end of the 1980s and the beginning of the 1990s, the responsibility for many aspects of personnel was being transferred from national prescribed procedures to locally-decided and managed procedures. This ranged from looking at the terms and conditions of employment to the particular skill mixes of people it was necessary to employ to do various jobs. It was anticipated that local personnel departments were going to have to move from administering other people's decisions to *managing* the personnel issues. There was an obvious incentive for personnel departments to get involved and assess where they were currently, as they had new work on the horizon. Another factor was the Government money on offer at this time for the training of personnel people in the health service.

So we had several advantages to get the project going. First, there was a clear, discrete group of people to decide the competencies for. Second, we actually knew something about these jobs before we started. Third, the group itself were aware they were going to have to change. Fourth, there was plenty of money around to pay for training and development after the competencies had been assessed. No wonder we got the list of competencies out within three months and individuals had started using it soon after and were involved in all sorts of development activities – the climate was right.

The basis of the model we developed was an analysis of the jobs that needed to be done by personnel managers. The following list, we felt, encompassed the main areas of expertise that a large NHS personnel department would need to have. The composite is based on the following eight facets of the personnel operational role:

1. The personnel manager as *selector*
2. The personnel manager as *paymaster*
3. The personnel manager as *negotiator*
4. The personnel manager as *performance monitor*
5. The personnel manager as *welfare worker*
6. The personnel manager as *human resource planner*
7. The personnel manager as *trainer*
8. The personnel manager as *communicator*

Every mainstream personnel management job consists of one or more of these roles. Selector and trainer are those most commonly found to comprise a complete job. Some combination of two or three is usual; all the roles are highly interdependent. We also proposed a list of generic competencies across jobs which were more or less necessary for each job holder. (See Chapter 5, Figure 5.6 for more details.)

There have been many criticisms of the type of analysis we were putting forward, not least of which is the belief that a competency-based approach cannot take into account individual differences.

'Users of competency based assessment should be aware that it provides one relatively partial view of performance. Its strong emphasis on the need for scientific rigour tends to lead to a rather

5

narrow perspective which, on its own, is barely capable of reflecting the rich and often paradoxical nature of human behaviour.'

Jacobs (1989)

One way around this problem is to construct competency analysis in terms of self assessment, enabling staff at all levels and varying from expert to novice to assess their own training needs. Our research also demonstrated that wide differences in practice between parts of the organisation supported this need for a flexible approach. Thus, it was quite inappropriate to have an 'ideal' model of, for example, a personnel department in a district health authority. These are some of the main differences we found between Health Service districts:

• the different levels of funding received
• the different skills and experience of the people
• the differing hierarchical position of personnel, including the relationship to the general manager
• the differing relationships with Region
• differing perceptions of the personnel role held by personnel directors, their staff and their colleagues
• the differing nature of the districts themselves: size, labour markets, medical specialisms, and so forth.

Certainly the people working in the personnel departments felt that this self assessment and composite model worked for them as it left them in charge and was flexible enough to work in differing situations.

The main points from this case study are:

1. How important it was to find a model of competencies which fitted the particular circumstances of each of the personnel departments.
2. The climate was ready for us to do the work so it went quickly.
3. The task was relatively self contained with an identifiable professional group to work with.

It takes longer than you think

The second case was with another health organisation, in this case a Healthcare Trust, which in 1992 had asked us – Lisa Butler, Janet Griffin and myself – to look at the management competencies of the clinical directorates. These were a new type of grouping within the health authority and nationally where, for example, maternity, obstetrics, gynaecology and paediatrics became one clinical directorate. Each directorate has its own managerial team with responsibility for its own budget and areas such as recruiting and developing staff.

We interviewed all those involved in directorates and the top management of the Trust. We shadowed a proportion of the clinical directors, care managers and business managers who were responsible for running the clinical directorates. We drew up a list of competencies needed within each directorate team and then reported. This was followed up with individual training profiles for each member of each directorate team, and opportunities for development and training were available. By 1994, this process had been going on for the two years since we were asked in, and the training and development had just begun.

Complex use of competencies such as this project can take a very long time! Here we were dealing with the following issues:

- a major cultural change for the health authority, particularly the doctors
- management competencies, always the most difficult competencies to define
- a period of changing personalities at the top of the organisation, where some important structural and strategic decisions were being made and changed.

This experience is perhaps more typical than the previous straightforward example.

Three roles had been identified to manage the clinical directorates: clinical director, care manager and business manager. There were variously two, three or four people filling these roles in the directorates making up the directorate team, for example some people were joint business/care manager and in other cases there were two care managers. The business managers and clinical directors were often fairly new to these roles, whereas generally the care managers had held similar posts for some time.

It was inappropriate to prescribe who should do what for all the directorates as skills and needs varied. However, within each directorate there was a need for clear roles. They needed to decide, between them, who does what, so they could work effectively as a team. We listed seventeen areas of management work that any directorate is likely to need done by the people working within it. We split these into five sections: Goals; Responsibilities; Organisation; Uncertainty; and People – giving the mnemonic GROUP (see Figure 1.1).

Figure 1.1
Management competencies in a health authority

Goals
- goal setting and strategy
- planning
- resources
- information systems
- finance

Responsibilities
- marketing
- monitoring and evaluation
- managing yourself
- change and innovation

Organisation
- policy and procedures
- day to day operations

Uncertainty
- communication
- power play
- credibility
- leadership

People
- people management and skill mix
- directorate team roles

It was also important to decide how this was to be coordinated. Normal methods for doing this are to have an organisation structure, job descriptions, structured meetings and procedures. There was room for clarification in this area. There is, of course, also a need to temper formal systems with informal methods but a degree of formal understanding and clarity of purpose can save hours of duplication, omission and frustration.

At the time we were doing our research, the development of clinical directorates in the Healthcare Trust were in a state of transition. Even how many directorates and the personnel of each were still matters of debate. Clearly they could not take on everything at once and be successful. An important task was to prioritise which of the changes to tackle first and the order of those to follow.

There were some real advantages in the Healthcare Trust being so well established. The security experienced by individuals knowing each other so well had enabled the place to keep going through a period of quite extraordinary change. However, if the directorates were to work, each of the job holders had new orientations to take on.

- Clinical directors (clinical consultants) had a major cultural change to make, from being in charge in their clinical work to managing through influence and consensus in their management work. As someone said, it was a bit like trying to herd cats. In competency terms these people had to become competent at working with people and influencing others rather than relying on their positions of authority.
- Care managers (nurses who were individually very well established in the authority) had to allow each other to develop new skills and a business orientation away from the clinical setting while maintaining their unteachable experience and their established skills of being 'in touch'. In competency terms, they had to become competent in such things as planning and formal monitoring systems.
- Business managers (administrators used to being 'go fors') had to take on a proactive approach to information, planning and budgeting as well as providing administrative support, to avoid becoming a dumping ground.

All these required developing new ways of working with each other which can be difficult when people know each other so

9

well. However, it did mean that the extremes of being fashionable for fashion's sake were likely to be avoided. Although new strategic responsibilities – the 'new world' – needed to be taken on, it was unlikely that the practical operations side of actually running a health service – the 'real world' – would be lost in such a well established organisation.

How any particular directorate divided the work would, appropriately, vary as the competencies of individuals were taken into consideration. Problems were anticipated when there were areas of management work not covered. Similarly, problems could arise where there was a lack of clarity over who was doing particular things. There were some areas that, clearly, each of the clinical directorate managers needed to develop competency in, for example, gaining credibility, communication, and managing oneself.

The advantage of using a competency approach to these issues is it enabled the individuals of the clinical directorate management teams to assess their own strengths and needs, and to work out what needed developing. The vocabulary and emphasis on behaviour appealed to the various professions who were having to work together. The major problem was the time it took to get started and the lack of time perceived by some individuals, particularly medical staff who took pride in their clinical abilities rather than these more generic competencies. Trying to get the balance between technical skills and knowledge and general competencies is a recurring issue for professional groups who take on managerial responsibilities.

The main points from this case study are:

1. How competencies can be used to clarify what is needed from teams and individuals when a major cultural change is going on.
2. Concentrating on competencies rather than previous qualifications and experience can be useful when different professions have to cooperate and share work.
3. Major reorganisations take time.

References

JACOBS, R. (1989) Getting the Measure of Management Competence *Personnel Management*, June, 32–7.

2

What is Going on Nationally?

The examples given at the end of Chapter 1 are part of a much wider debate in the UK about how Government, employers and education establishments can work together to enhance the job-related skills of the working population. The economic significance of this cooperation is increasingly important because of changes in the content and organisation of work, changes that are driven partly by developments in technology but also by much more.

Increasing competitive pressures, particularly from overseas international companies, are forcing firms to adopt market strategies with an increased emphasis on product quality and customer focused products. Resulting production techniques – with their increased worker discretion, management structures which are flatter, and increased decentralisation – all highlight the importance of skills and competencies in the workplace. They also raise questions about how adequate current arrangements are to generate these skills and competencies.

There is also pressure to use competencies from within the European Union. All Europeans have the right to travel across EU borders for work and this has led to a desire for an equivalence between qualifications. Traditionally, Britain has had a more informal system of qualifications than many other countries, particularly Germany. In Spain, for example, when electrical work is done in a house, the electrician issues a certificate to say they have done the work and that it is safe. Only those who have the appropriate qualifications can get and issue these certificates. In the UK there are electricians working with varying levels of qualifications, but equally there are individuals doing electrical repairs who have no formal qualifications; and no certificates of safe installation are expected or given. Using competencies as the basis for national qualifications, and then equivalence across borders, alleviates the difficulties of differences between job titles and cultures, as competencies concentrate on the ability to do the job. A central European agency, based in Berlin, has been set up to encourage this equivalence. It is called CEDEFOP which translates into English as, the European Centre for the Development of Vocational Training.

In recent years Central Government in the UK has devoted considerable energy and invested large amounts of money in exhorting employers and educational establishments to develop closer links. Through such links it is hoped that the secondary and further education which takes place will be more suited to the skills required by employers. The Government has also set up a range of schemes for schools, colleges and universities to encourage these links. Recent examples include Compacts, Technical and Vocational Education Initiatives (TVEI), Records of Achievement, Integrated Graduate Development schemes, the High Technology National Training Scheme, and Enterprise in Higher Education. The Government has also encouraged European Union programmes such as COMETT and EuroPACE that help industry and universities to work closer together.

The importance of using education facilities as well as in-house training to enhance workers' competencies is more than just the availability of the institutions. In a report to the OECD (Organisation for Economic Cooperation and Development) Keith Drake (1991) points out that universities have a unique contribution to make to the continuing development of personnel as they, unlike employers or Central Government, are inclined to put the learning process at the centre of their model of economic life. Judith Marquand (1989) points out how important this is by arguing that, though the UK's industrial culture does not accord this central position to learning, there is no good organisational or economic reason why it should not do so, and there are very strong competitive reasons to justify learning being placed in that way. The willingness of many employers, both large and small, to get involved in the various schemes listed above suggests that many are now feeling this to be so.

The explosive growth of knowledge in the last few decades could mean a greater emphasis in higher education on acquiring this knowledge through cramming information, greater specialisation, earlier specialisation or less emphasis on developing the ability to learn. The debate in education circles revolves around whether such a response is appropriate or whether the emphasis should be less on *what* is learned and more on the training of minds for the *process* of learning and self development. This is reflected in the competency movement, where lists of competencies often, but not always, include self development, learning skills and self management.

Once the preferred nature of the learning – knowledge or ability to learn – is established, this learning is assessed and recorded, which leads to yet another area of current debate. The Government has made a strong push to try to coordinate all assessment and recording under the National Vocational Qualification (NVQ) system. NVQs are competency based and currently have levels ranging from basic to equivalent to higher education awards in some vocational areas.

This background debate about training and education, and the relationships between Government, employers and education inevitably also involves a great deal of analysis and discussion by those involved. They are often concerned with the power and permission structures involved in how things are changed, rather than the actual content of the competencies and how they should be assessed. It is against this lively background that we look at the use of competencies.

The national scene on training

Since the mid 1980s an enormous amount of time, energy and money has been spent on the issue of training by the British Government and other organisations. This has been due, in part, to pressure from the European Union but also to a hope that a better training of the British workforce will improve four main issues:

1. A relatively declining economic position.
2. Dealing with the rapid change in technologies.
3. Changing patterns of employment and consequently unemployment.
4. A dissatisfaction with education provision which is seen as having not provided suitably skilled workers for employers.

For these and other reasons there have been a large number of training and training-related initiatives, with various initials and abbreviations. It can be quite a minefield of exclusive jargon. Perhaps the most important for general management purposes are NETTs, NVQs, and TECs and LECs.

National Education and Training Targets (NETTs) are nationally set targets for young people and adults to be reached by the year 2000 (see Figure 2.1). It is assumed that employers will play a large part in this and they are encouraged to do so through the Government-sponsored initiative 'Investors in People'.

Figure 2.1
National Education and Training Targets (NETTs)
up to the year 2000

NATIONAL EDUCATION AND TRAINING TARGETS
FOUNDATION LEARNING

- By 1997, 80% of young people to reach NVQ 2 (or equivalent)
- Training and education to NVQ 3 (or equivalent) available to all young people who can benefit
- By 2000, 50% of young people to reach NVQ 3 (or equivalent)
- Education and training provision to develop self-reliance, flexibility and breadth

NATIONAL EDUCATION AND TRAINING TARGETS
LIFETIME LEARNING

- By 1996, all employees to take part in training or development activities
- By 1996, 50% of the workforce aiming for NVQs or units towards them
- By 2000, 50% of the workforce qualified to at least NVQ 3 (or equivalent)
- By 1996, 50% of medium to larger organisations to be 'Investors in People'

National Vocational Qualifications (NVQs) range from level 1, basic, to level 5, professional and managerial. They cover a wide variety of vocations and professions and are given by a large number of organisations who have been validated by the National Vocational Council. The Government's aim is to make them the main vocational qualifications, with professional and craft qualifications tied into the system. NVQs are a framework of qualifications designed by each industry to focus on the skills and knowledge used in jobs. They are awarded by major national awarding bodies such as City and Guilds, and RSA. Within the NVQ framework there are qualifications for jobs at different levels of responsibility and complexity, from foundation skills at level 1 up to senior management at level 5. NVQs are not examinations or courses but qualifications you gain by demonstrating to a qualified assessor that you can carry out activities at work to a national standard of performance. An assessor may observe the performance in a work situation or use evidence of recent skills and experiences to make a judgement about competency. NVQs are made up of units of work activity which can be individually assessed and certified as new skills are developed.

There is no direct equivalence between NVQ levels and job titles and salaries as these are often based on tradition, scarcity of skills and political power rather than competencies. One problem of trying to attach job titles to different NVQ levels is that what is meant by the titles varies from employer to employer. Indeed, the strength of the NVQ system is that it is *not* dependent on interpreting job titles. When one looks at a particular job role there can often be a profile of competencies from different levels such as business information level 2 and customer service level 3. However, to give you some idea of the feel of the levels, here are some approximate examples for guidance:

Level 1   Filing clerk
Level 2   Administration assistant
Level 3   Secretary
Level 4   Office manager
Level 5   Office services manager

Another example is the different levels of engineering skills of Foundry and Casting:

Level 1   Diecasting

15

Level 2   Includes the above and some pattern making
Level 3   Includes all the above and pattern moulding, pattern making and model making
Level 4   General engineering manufacture which includes the above and testing and planning

The Management NVQs are part of the MCI (Management Charter Initiative) and work in exactly the same way, starting with level 1 which is equivalent to NVQ 4. Currently there are MCI standards for junior management and middle management, with an expectation of a level 3 for senior management in the future.

Accreditation of prior learning (APL) is a way of getting credit in the form of units within an NVQ for the skills and experience that already exist. This means there is no need to do a course or relearn what is already known to receive recognition of abilities. It is up to the individual to present evidence of how they perform the different tasks to the national standard. Evidence can be collected from a variety of sources including: presenting examples of work to an assessor, asking the employer to write a letter which confirms the skills, requesting an assessor to come and observe the person carrying out tasks in a work situation. Advice and support about APL and NVQs are available from qualified APL advisers at local TECs.

Training and Enterprise Councils (TECs) and Local Enterprise Companies in Scotland (LECs) were set up by the Department of Employment and the Scottish Office to involve local employers in improving the skills base in their area. The boards are made up from local chief executives of commercial firms and a few public-sector stakeholders such as Further and Higher Education establishments. The TECs and LECs are also charged with managing various government initiatives such as youth and adult training.

These various initiatives, and others, have raised the profile of training, and the competency approach to training in particular, on a national level.

The role of professional bodies

Another set of important stakeholders nationally concerned with training and competencies are the professional bodies. When an organisation employs professionals a lot of the issues about competency are traditionally addressed through the professional body. At the heart of the professions is the issue of having a licence to practise. Some are closed professions, with only licenced practitioners practising, others are open where anyone can practise. Science and engineering tend to be closed professions, whereas management – notoriously – is an open profession. The basis for licensing in closed professions has usually been to insure individuals who deal with the public or because there are serious safety issues involved. Clearly, the very process of licensing for a closed profession makes for a regulatory body which controls minimum training standards.

No formal list exists in Britain of the professions. Vaughan (1991) suggests bodies which may be considered to represent professions vary in several ways. They might be regulating, or not; they can have degree entry, or not. Some have a policy on continuing professional development (CPD) and whether it should be recorded, others do not.

Our current focus on competencies and the issue of continuing professional development is important. For members of professional bodies it is an important influence on the level of competency over time. Increasingly professions are emphasising CPD and particularly credit bearing CPD. There are important questions to ask about CPD.

Questions to ask yourself

Should there be CPD
  – from the individual's point of view?
  – from the employer's point of view?

What does 'mandatory/required' mean when it appears in professional bodies' rules for continuing membership which are dependent upon CPD?
  – maintaining log books?
  – making sure time is available to do CPD?
  – some judging of professional output?

Should the professions facilitate, prescribe or control the CPD?

How does this fit in with NVQs, MCI and the employers' own lists of competencies?

From an organisation's point of view, in the understanding of competencies nationally it is well worth trying to understand what is going on in the professional bodies of those who work for the organisation. The most obvious profession to take as an example is engineering, as engineers are one of the most widely employed group of professionals. They are controlled by various institutions of engineering who are coordinated by the Engineering Council. In his report on the professions, Vaughan (1991) points out that the role of the Engineering Council is wider than just engineering, especially in continuing education and training (CET). The Engineering Council offers competency-based qualifications through the various institutions of engineering. The sequence of qualifying is normally:

1. The degree must come from an accredited institution, inspected by the appropriate institution of engineering.
2. The student becomes a graduate member.
3. The student then becomes an associate member after two–three years of practical experience and the submission of an experience report or 'log book'.
4. The student becomes a chartered engineer, after supervisory or management experience, approximately three or four years later.
5. The institutes control the standards and the chartering process.
6. The qualifications are professionally recognised internationally.

This is not just a self-satisfying process for individuals. Employers also feel the chartering process is important. For example, the resources manager for a large electronics company, when asked how important it is to be chartered, replied:

It is becoming more so, because of the 1992 syndrome. Engineers on the Continent are revered like doctors. They have social standing; for example a chartered engineer can sign passports. We do a lot of work on the Continent. It is a competitive market. We need quality people. We have few chartered engineers at the moment, and few members of the IEE (Institution of Electrical Engineers), because of the lack of incentives in the company. Progression is irrespective of qualifications. We sell our company as a technical company. This causes no problems while we operate in the UK, the problem arises in Europe. We need encouragement,

such as monetary bonuses. We don't even pay institute membership fees at the moment. It is hard to encourage individuals when
there is no light at the end of the tunnel.

The development of interest in competencies

The competency movement was greatly influenced by the German
technical training schemes which inspired the European Union's
training movement. This in turn influenced the British Government
departments and particularly the Employment Department's off-
shoot, Training, Enterprise and Education Division (TEED).
TEED have been made responsible for developing interest in
NVQs and competency-based training nationally. The Government's argument is that the national competency-based qualifications, NVQs, make individuals more effective as employees but
also more independent of organisations and professional bodies,
hence creating a more flexible workforce. Another strand in the
development of interest in competencies came from the USA with
the management competency movement, for example, Boyatzis's
(1982) very influential book, *The Competent Manager.*

The earlier background of competency is in psychology and
the ability to describe and measure behaviours. In organisations
this has been used to concentrate attention on what jobs need
doing and whether a person can do them. For example, job
assessment and job evaluation techniques, systematic training,
and assessment centres have all used behavioural analysis and
competency assessment as the basis for discrimination between
jobs and individuals. Some of these techniques go back as far as
the Second World War when the British Government used 'house
parties' to select senior staff for the Army and Civil Service.

The early 1990s have seen a born-again fervour in the UK
towards competencies. Government agencies, such as TEED and
TECs, are under a lot of pressure to get people to introduce competency-based schemes. The people of TEED have targets to
meet, performance-related pay associated with these targets, and
the individuals employed by TEED have temporary contracts.
(There can be a somewhat frantic feel to some discussions about
competencies when the targets are not being met.) Similarly, in
organisations, there are individuals in training departments who

19

have singled out a competency approach as *the* way forward, reaching a religious zeal on occasions.

There is no 'profession of competency' but there are certainly, nationally and locally, individuals whose working life is dedicated to promoting the use of competencies. Some people are completely hooked on the idea of being able to analyse, describe and assess all behaviours necessary to achieve organisational success. They feel it is only a matter of getting effort and ability applied to the subject and then excellence will be achieved. Others constitutionally feel that the world is a rather more uncertain and messy place and that some aspects of the human condition, including parts of organisational life, cannot be described in behavioural terms. Where an individual fits along this range is as much a matter of personality and ideology as reasoned argument. This is a familiar dichotomy in psychology circles, between behaviourists and other schools of psychology, and has never been resolved to everyone's satisfaction.

Inevitably, displays of certainty such as some of the competency professionals have given have led to widespread scepticism. Some of this has just been a natural suspicion of 'right answers'. Some of it has come from an alignment of vested interests such as professional bodies and educational establishments who have well established training and assessment procedures that are not necessarily competency based. We also need to be aware of individual organisations which are following fashion and going along with competencies in the hope of improving performance, without really applying the effort required to effect change. In the practical world of trying to improve the competencies of people and organisations, it probably pays to be pragmatic. Use the bits that work and leave the academic niceties to those who enjoy the debate.

Vocabulary

Like all good professions, social science can get very enmeshed in the precise use of vocabulary. It keeps many of us occupied for weeks. Some of it is entirely pedantic, while some of the distinctions are more useful as they try to analyse the ideological differences and separate assumptions that people are making in their use of particular words. The development of the competency movement is no exception; it has had an allied industry of linguistic expertise. Hours of passionate debate go into such niceties as the difference between competence and competency, a difference Reid et al., for example feel they need to distinguish:

> In this text we have used the term 'competence' in relation to the 'outcomes' approach and the term 'competency' with reference to the 'input' approach.
>
> Reid et al. (1992) p. 237

For the most part these distinctions are really not so critical for the practitioner and so I have not made the distinctions in this book. But where an apparently rarefied abstract debate means real differences in practice, I have sought to clarify the issues involved. For example, the debate about how specific or general to draw competencies will determine how prescriptive the list is. Very detailed lists leave little room for manoeuvre for the individual who may, consequently, feel very controlled and want to 'work to rule'. Very general lists allow plenty of freedom for the individual but give little clue as to what is meant by competent performance.

Competency is about performance – how we define it, assess it, develop it, acquire it and so on. Some desired performances, or competencies, are easy to define, measure and develop. For example, anything which requires physical effort can be observed; anything which has a physical outcome can be measured. This might include such things as digging ditches, getting the car to start, doing pirouettes. However, many desired performances or competencies are much more complex and are difficult to observe or measure. For example, anything which requires the cooperation of other people to achieve; anything where the effectiveness of the performance depends on the judgement of others. This might include such things as negotiating trade agreements, attracting people to come into a restaurant, ensuring that governors come to governors' meetings. But even in these difficult to judge areas we can usually agree that some individuals' performance is more effective than that of others. The competency question is, 'What are they doing which makes them competent?'

What the competency movement tries to do is to analyse what

it is that makes some people's performance better than others and to list the component factors which go to make up these competent performances. Where this involves relatively simple physical competencies there is usually little difference except over how much detail is required. However, once unobservable characteristics are included we start to get passionate debate about what makes up the competent performance. Add to this the debate about how much detail to go into, and whether this is more or less controlling than desired, and you can begin to understand why the academic and professional press is full of articles about competency. For our purposes – developing the use of competencies in-house – the decisions about what to include in any list of desired competencies for a particular performance really only need to involve those within the organisation who have a legitimate say in that performance.

It is the analysis of what behaviours, skills, knowledge, understanding and personal qualities go to make up a competent performance that is at the heart of using a competency approach. It is the reference to the work-based performance which is the critical distinction between this approach and many others.

Management competencies

As an example of the general issues involved in using the competency approach, let us look briefly at management competency. Management is particularly useful to look at, partly because so much is written about management, partly because management is about power and control, and partly because management is a vague concept which has led to management competencies attracting a great deal of passionate debate. Trying to agree a list of management competencies which are neither too general and obvious nor too specific, prescriptive and controlling is an interesting exercise – as the organisers of the Management Charter Initiative (MCI), the NVQ body for management, have found out.

The management competency movement became very popular in the UK in the late 1980s and has remained so. It is hoped that by looking at management competencies we can improve management performance by making training and recruitment more appropriate. The approach is also being used to measure management performance.

Management competencies are taken to mean more than just the skills necessary to do the job; they are seen as clusters of skills, knowledge and values. Lists of competencies can also include personal attributes, such as self-confidence, and mind sets, such as pro-activity. Three writers have been most influential in this area, Boyatzis (1982) from the USA and Burgoyne and Stuart (1976) in the UK. The competencies in most studies are based on observations, interviews and statistical evaluation of the material gathered. The competency approach emphasises that there is more than one way of being an effective or competent manager. It emphasises that instead of training managers in just a particular technique we need to consider a variety of ways of developing the various competencies.

The temptation for those responsible for management performance and development is to rush in and use these lists of clusters to measure management performance. This is particularly likely to happen where there is pressure to make people accountable and when there is some form of performance-related pay in operation. Each organisation is encouraged to apply the clusters to their own staff to find the particular management abilities statistically associated with good performance. However, some of the material on management competencies can be based on a vary narrow definition of what management is about and may not be appropriate for your needs. This does not mean you should not use them, but you should use them with some sense of proportion. Two useful review articles about management competencies are by Stewart (1990) and Jacobs (1989).

The problems of introducing national competency schemes

Most of this book is about developing competencies within a particular organisation but this chapter has been looking at the broader national scene. Therefore, I conclude this chapter by noting some of the particular problems associated with developing national schemes of competency and their assessment processes.

There are several different stakeholders and interest groups influencing the standards maintained for formal qualifications.

23

These include the Government, the Lead Bodies, professional bodies, the universities, the national and international academic community, and employer preferences as articulated by employers' groups such as the Confederation of British Industry (CBI). The NCVQ (National Council for Vocational Qualifications), its Scottish equivalent and MCI need to find their place alongside these.

MCI has not been widely and enthusiastically taken up by the professional management bodies, the industrial community, or elsewhere in education. This may be due to inertia, intransigence or poor publicity. On the other hand, it may be at least partly due to fundamental flaws in its conception and design. It takes a long time to get to grips with the MCI material. Other similar materials, such as the Institution of Civil Engineers' (1992), are much more accessible. Until general acceptance reaches a higher level, a positive response from organisations is unlikely.

The cost of introducing national competencies

You may decide to use the national assessment qualifications as the basis for your competencies, in which case you will use a local assessor for each NVQ to moderate what you are doing. But there are significant costs in both time and resources when introducing a competency-based system. Whether the new system is worth it – or whether it is even possible – must be assessed. Here are some comments from people I interviewed who have experience of introducing a competency-based system.

A director of continuing education and training described the *information costs* of becoming too variable.

> 'The dangers of APL (accreditation of prior learning) lie in the information costs and the reliability and validity of the assessment. We are in trouble if it becomes all about soft qualifications. We must take heed of the American experience where *where* you got the qualification is far more important than *what* qualification you got . . . It is no good if no one has an idea what the qualification means.'

A training officer explained the *costs of time* when using the national assessment procedures for NVQs called APL.

'I have just done an APL and it is extremely time-consuming and expensive. There is a need to resource this assessing but also to resource for the time to fill in the sheets.'

The management training and development officer for an electricity supply company had the following to say about *costs*.

'You'll find a lot of companies who thought NVQs were a good idea to start with, but who are now dropping it. They cost too much and take too much time.'

A lecturer in mechanical engineering worried about the *bureaucracy* which would be involved.

'I really worry about the bureaucracy of all this. Engineering needs to be simplified, because it still turns people off. It has got to be simple. We have to trust people to say "this person has passed", rather than endlessly looking through all the evidence.'

These are issues for the national bodies to resolve if NVQs are to become the normal basis of assessment of competency. You need to decide whether to use national schemes, develop your own or create some sort of hybrid. The rest of this book discusses the development of a competency approach within an organisation to suit the people and purposes of that specific organisation.

References

BOYATZIS, R. E. (1982) *The Competent Manager: A model for Effective Performance*, John Wiley and Sons, New York

BURGOYNE, J. G. and STUART, R. (1976) The Nature, Use and Acquisition of Managerial Skills and Other Attributes *Personnel Review*, **5** (4) 19–29

DRAKE, K. (1991) Higher Education and Employment: the Changing Relationship, in *Recent Developments in Continuing Professional Development*, Organisation for Economic Co-operation and Development, Paris

Institution of Civil Engineers (1992) *Management Development in the Construction Industry: Guidelines for the Professional Engineer*, Thomas Telford, London

JACOBS, R. (1989) Getting the Measure of Management Competence *Personnel Management*, June, 32–7

MARQUAND, J. (1989) *Autonomy and Change: The Sources of Economic Growth*, Harvester Wheatsheaf, London

REID, M. A., BARRINGTON, H. and KENNEY, J. (1992) *Training Interventions: Managing Employee Development*, 3rd edn, IPM, London

STEWART, R. (1990) What is Happening to Middle Managers? *British Journal of Management*, Spring, 3–16

VAUGHAN, P. (1991) *Maintaining Professional Competence*, University of Hull Press

3

Do I Want to Measure Competency Organisation-wide?

This chapter and the next look at a variety of different reasons why organisations and hence the people working in them might want to get involved with competencies. There are also good reasons why individuals may want to get involved for purely personal benefits. Kanter (1989) has argued that in the future job security will not be based on people working for the same organisation all their working lives but on each individual's *employability*.

'If security no longer comes from being employed, then it must come from being employable.

In a post-entrepreneurial era in which corporations need flexibility to change and restructuring is a fact of life, the promise of very long-term employment security would be the wrong one to expect employers to make. But employability security – the knowledge that today's work will enhance the person's value in terms of future opportunities – that is a promise that can be made and kept. Employability security comes from the chance to accumulate human capital – skills and reputation – that can be invested in new opportunities as they arise.'

Kanter (1989) p. 321

If Kanter is right it suggests that individuals should constantly keep up to date with skills and knowledge, and learn to *learn*. She also implies that organisations will need employees who can take on new ideas and techniques and adapt to situations which match their (often dynamic) core activities. One approach to this matching of skills of the individual with needs of the organisation is through the use of competency analysis.

The general methodology underlying the competency approach offers organisations access to a more formal, structured and reliable framework for assessing and developing staff than some previous approaches. It also gives individuals transferable accreditation for their competency acquired both at work and in educational establishments. Indeed, it can even include credit for competencies acquired at home, as some people are finding when they are assessed and gain NVQs after years away from education and paid employment.

Competencies are being used by organisations in a wide range of ways, for anything remotely affecting performance. It is used by different people to mean different things. It can be used for job specific, easily assessible skills or for complex, core competencies. This chapter and Chapter 4 look at some different reasons organisations may get involved with the competency approach. This is not just because it seems to me the logical thing to do. Clarifying the purpose of using competencies can help identify the scale, the methodology and the resources required to implement the scheme. Time spent at the beginning deciding why we are getting involved can prevent getting bogged down later, when we may find people are working with different assumptions or changing the purpose as they go along. This clarifying of the purpose may sometimes lead to the conclusion that now is not the time to get involved because other things need clarifying or doing first. In this and the succeeding chapters I raise some of the questions you need to consider, both before getting involved and once you are involved.

One common starting point for using competencies is to ensure that the personnel of the organisation are competent in those areas which are important to the organisation. At this stage questions need to be asked.

Questions to ask yourself

What do we want to do?

What are we doing?

Have we got the staff now who can do it?

Do we have access to sufficient good staff for the future?

A detailed competencies approach is one way of answering these questions, but only after some strategic and manpower decisions have been taken. Competencies is a methodical system for looking at the behaviour of individuals that fits in with some of the other systematic processes of management. It is conventional, and seems appropriate if we want to be systematic, to start with the overall organisation and then work through to the individual.

Strategic management

The word 'strategy' is a semantic minefield; people use the term in all sorts of ways and often imply several different uses in the same statement. Mintzberg et al. (1988) suggest there are five different uses of the term: plan, ploy, pattern, position and perspective.

- Usually strategy is a *plan* – that is, a consciously intended course of action.
- It can also be used as a *ploy* – that is a manoeuvre to outwit competitors.
- Strategy can also be a *pattern* which is inferred from consistent behaviour to suggest that someone, usually a competitor, has a strategy.
- Depending where you sit, different things will be strategic; so *position* is important as an expression of the environment and, by definition, the strategy identifies that position.
- Strategy is a concept or *perspective* – the important thing is that, within an organisation, people share the perspective.

Mintzberg et al. maintain that these five different uses are not necessarily conflicting, indeed they can be complementary, but that more careful use of the term may avoid some of the confusions which so often occur when people are talking about strategy.

Most of this section uses the word strategy in the sense of planning. That is, the process of deciding priorities, setting targets, and agreeing the main purposes of the business, section, division or unit. It may include short-, medium- and long-term goals. It is likely to include some changes which have been imposed from outside but have been tuned to local conditions. The ability to monitor various environments, seek out and synthesise multiple sources and types of information, and develop and implement a plan of action that anticipates trends before

29

they are obvious is one of the most useful competencies of senior staff.

Thompson and Strickland (1990) describe the five tasks of strategic management as a continuous process which starts with defining the business, getting specific performance objectives, deciding how to achieve the objectives, and ends with implementing and evaluating the performance – and then the whole process is recycled.

Strategic planning

Strategic planning is having a clear sense of direction and focusing on where the business is going. Although obvious, this simple clarification and possible change in emphasis can have a profound effect. For instance, when the management of Canadian Pacific Railway decided that they were not in the business of running a railway but in the business of transportation, they saw ways of developing rather than managing decline. From such a clear sense of direction can stem specific objectives: the collation of necessary information, the anticipation of problems, and the assessment of strengths, weaknesses and opportunities.

The planning process is basically concerned with the following questions.

Questions to ask yourself

Where do we want to be?

Where are we now?

How do we get there?

How are we doing?

There are, of course, more sophisticated models of strategic management (see Moore 1992 for a useful summary of these). Using the simple framework provided by the above questions or perhaps another, more complex model, strategic and business planning can be undertaken. Planning can be short term – for immediate, this year, changes – or it can be for longer-term prospects, such as developing a service over five years.

No organisation can ignore the environment in which it operates. Porter (1980 and 1985) developed his classic model to describe the four forces of competition which make up the environment of an organisation:

- the threat of new entrants
- the threat of substitute products
- the bargaining power of buyers
- the bargaining power of suppliers.

Strategic management is mostly about trying to defend the organisation from these forces or trying actively to influence them. The balance between them will vary over time, place and circumstance. For example, legislation on pollution may well prohibit new entrants to the business so reducing the threat of increasing competition, whereas a reduction in the number of buyers, for example house purchasers because of a recession, reduces the price organisations can charge – in this case, house builders. Similarly, the purchase of a new scanner in one hospital may substitute the need to use the old style scanner at another health trust hospital. All these could affect the strategy of businesses in these markets.

A typical sequence for the planning process used in both public- and private-sector organisations in the UK is:

- establishing the mission
- internal and external analysis
- setting objectives
- developing actionable strategies
- integration of the plan
- providing appropriate controls
- evaluation measures
- review.

There are dangers in an overemphasis on strategic planning; it can become the purpose of the organisation rather than an aid to running the business. Thought is no substitute for action, plans are not an alternative to doing, and analysis can aid but never replace judgement.

Currently, the advantages of strategic planning probably outweigh the disadvantages for most types of organisation, but there are notes of caution being sounded by those who feel that entrepreneurial flair can be stifled by an over-preoccupation with analysis (see, for example, Peters and Austin, 1985). It is also one of the well known paradoxes of strategic management (see Quinn, 1980, or Lindblom, 1959) that large, well-managed organisations constantly change their strategies in small ways rather than adopting a grand model for all time (as recommended in some of the management literature).

Core competencies and strategic management

The 1990s have seen an increasing interest in, and emphasis on, the behavioural aspects of strategy in contrast to the traditional structural model (see, for example, Prahalad and Hamel, 1990 and Stalk, Evans and Shulman, 1992). This is in part because analysis of organisations shows that companies that are good at one thing, such as getting new products to market, tend to be good at other things as well. For example, successful companies tend to be good at responding to customer complaints, their product quality is consistent, they have insight into customer needs. They also have the ability to exploit markets and to enter new businesses; they generate new ideas and innovate. These qualities are seen as reflections of a more fundamental characteristic called core competency or capabilities-based competition. This approach acknowledges that the success of an organisation involves more than just allocating money in the short term, but relies on the skills, or competencies, of the people who comprise the organisation.

Prahalad and Hamel (1990) define core competency as the combination of individual technologies and production skills that underlies a company's myriad product lines. For example, Sony's core competency is miniaturisation which allows them to make everything from Walkmans to video cameras to notebook computers. These core competencies explain the ease with which successful companies are able to enter new, and seemingly unrelated businesses. In the short term a company's competitiveness derives from the price/performance attributes of current products.

In the long term it derives from an ability to build at lower cost and speedily, unanticipated products spawned by the core competencies:

'First, a core competence provides potential access to a wide variety of markets . . . Second, a core competence should make a significant contribution to the perceived customer benefits of the end product . . . Finally, a core competence should be difficult for competitors to imitate. And it *will* be difficult if it is a complex harmonisation of individual technologies and production skills.'
Prahalad and Hamel (1990) pp. 83–4

Stalk et al. (1992) use the phrase 'capabilities-based' instead of 'core competencies'. They place more emphasis on the processes operating within the organisation than the technologies and skills. They are not identical concepts but the niceties of the distinction do not need to concern us here. Stalk et al. (p. 62) suggest that the four basic principles of capabilities-based competition are

1. The building blocks of corporate strategy are not products and markets but business processes.
2. Competitive success depends on transforming a company's key processes into strategic capabilities that consistently provide superior value to the customer.
3. Companies create these capabilities by making strategic investments in a support infrastructure that links together and transcends traditional SBUs (strategic business units) and functions.
4. Because capabilities necessarily cross functions, the champion of a capabilities-based strategy is the CEO (chief executive officer).

Stalk et al. (1992) p. 62

Kay (1993) also takes this process approach to strategy and emphasises the behavioural attributes to success. He is critical of how strategic writing emphasises military models of vision and leadership, size and share. He argues that the task of developing a strategy is identifying the firm's distinctive capabilities from among the following four ingredients and relating them to the environment:

- Architecture or the network of relational contracts within or around the firm.
- Reputation which is the customers' guide to aspects of quality that.the company cannot monitor for themselves and is only of value in a continuing market.
- Innovation, although establishing the competitive edge is often difficult.
- Strategic assets, which may be monopolies or due to regulation.

Identifying these distinctive capabilities would, in our vocabulary, give the organisations core competencies.

Identifying core strategic competencies

At the heart of identifying the core competencies of an organisation are the decisions top management have to make and these involve strategic decisions. This process is largely outside the scope of this book. Briefly, it involves looking dispassionately at the organisation's business and deciding what it is really about.

Questions to ask yourself?

What are we good at?

What skills, processes, relationships, technology make us good at this?

What makes us different from others in this business?

What could we not do without in the future?

To do these things, what do we need?

Have a think about what processes and relations, as well as products, are critical to your organisation.

Questions to ask yourself

How long would we keep our competitiveness if we did not control this particular core competency?

How central is this core competency to perceived customer benefits?

What future opportunities would disappear if we were to lose this core competency?

Do we ask managers to compete for the organisation's cash but never for key, talented people?

Will the proposed project/product/development contribute to efficient asset accumulation, including competency?

This strategic process of identifying core competencies may be your starting point for getting involved with competencies.

This book is about individual competencies and how to describe, assess and develop them but these fundamental questions are a good starting point as they help concentrate on the real business of the organisation and keeps the competency list focused on this.

Core strategic competencies and the individual employee

In many organisations, some of the core competencies of the organisation are individually controlled. For example, hospital departments rely on the reputation of particular consultants to attract patients. Similarly, hairdressing salons rely on particular stylists for their reputation. This dependence is often reflected in contracts which forbid individuals who leave from practising their trade within several miles of their previous employment. Some manufacturing organisations are also, finally, beginning to realise their dependence on technically competent individuals and are introducing reward systems of pay and status commensurate with management scales for technical people. One example of an organisation doing this is the computer company ICL who are giving status and financial rewards to experts (*Financial*

Times, October 29 1993, p. 14). But not all cases are so clear-cut. The relationship between the organisation and the individual has kept management experts and social scientists occupied for years (see Morgan 1986 for an excellent review of the area). The balance between the organisation's competency and the individual's competency is an interesting one, particularly in a period of changing relationships as described by Kanter at the beginning of this chapter. One issue is whether the organisation needs to nurture a core group of employees who are well trained, developed and appropriately paid. These people are expected to be committed to the organisation and work long hours for their rewards. Other workers are seen as periphery and employed when the demands are there and discarded at other times. Little commitment is made to their development and, equally, little commitment is expected from them.

> *Questions to ask yourself*
>
> Do we need a core group of competent individuals who ensure the core competencies of the organisation?
>
> Can we depend on a periphery workforce of contractors, and temporary and part-time employees?
>
> Where do we buy-in competent performers from? Education, competitors, recruitment agencies?

Lowendahl (1993) in a study of strategic management in professional business service firms, such as engineering design, management consultancy and insurance brokerage, found that the relationship between the competencies of the organisation and the individuals working in the organisation could lead to differing outcomes (see Figure 3.1). If this model applies elsewhere, then the continuing success of an organisation depends not only on identifying the core competencies but also on developing individual competencies to match these.

Figure 3.1
Relationship between organisation and individual competency

Organisational competency

	LOW	HIGH
HIGH	People-based, highly vulnerable to exits	Balanced expertise and organisational maturity
LOW	Unlikely to survive	Routine- or model-based, highly vulnerable to obsolescence

Individual competency (row label spanning the left side)

Source: Lowendahl, 1993

One way this happens is by building competency through the contracts won and services delivered, so individuals develop as the contracts are done. A more systematic way for large organisations is to plan ahead, predicting what the organisation is going to need and investing in the people who work in the organisation to develop them to meet anticipated needs.

Systematic Human Resource Management

One aspect of an increased interest in the behavioural aspects of strategic management has been corresponding interest in attempting to match the way people are developed and managed to fit them to meet the organisational aims – generally known as

Human Resource Management (HRM). Several large and small organisations have been making efforts to integrate comprehensive systematic human resource management approaches. This is rather easier to achieve in a new 'greenfield' company than in a well established setting with a variety of historically based customs and practices – with an ingrained organisational 'culture'. However, several large, well established organisations have had a go (see, for example, Storey, 1992). The idea is to coordinate all aspects of managing individuals and what they do with the planned activity of the organisation, including developing people for the company's future goals. In a perfect, simple system their answer to the following questions would be yes.

Questions to ask yourself

Have we got a *strategic* plan?

Is there a central *human resource* plan, possibly based on core strategic competencies?

Do we know our *human resource* plan, identifying what sorts of jobs need doing now and will need doing in the future to deliver the plan?

What about a *recruitment* and induction plan to meet future needs?

Is there an *appraisal* system in place to identify where staff are up to in their development?

Do we manage *performance*, including soft and hard attributes, to motivate staff?

Have we got a *training and development* plan to develop current staff?

In this sort of scheme, the identification of the organisation's core competencies would lead to an analysis of what would be required to deliver these, and then move on to ensuring that the people with the appropriate competency were in place.

One company I visited, a large chemical company, had spent a lot of time trying to get various human resource initiatives to come together in a common theme. They had eight underlying principles:

1. A single attitude to employment and work.
   'Every employee is part of a total business team.'
2. Work organised in the most effective way.
3. Jobs evaluated by consistent criteria.
   'Taking account of the requirements of the job and its contribution to the business.'
4. Fully informed staff.
5. Fully trained staff.
6. Opportunities for personal and career development.
7. Managers responsible for their staff.
8. Reward for merit and performance.

The employee relations manager of this company told me:

> 'The eight principles are vitally important and underpin how we manage jobs. They give management a common language and focus. For example, performance appraisal, career development and training should all be aiming towards the same ends. It gives people 'hooks to hang things on', it provides a common framework. It is a simple thing to buy into. It was originally driven by personnel and then devolved down to line managers.'

He continued by saying:

> 'We want to cut out fringe benefits/payments. We are looking to compete in a world market so performance management needs to be clear in purpose and organisation. Rewards must reinforce what is directed, so we need a reward system of great simplicity. We need to link rewards to medium- and long-term, soft and hard objectives . . .
>
> TQ (Total Quality) process is the glue that ties everything else together because it gives us a common language and values to subscribe to. For example, systematic improvement is continuous. It frees individuals to contribute ideas and effort to the organisation. It is the background process to accelerate others. Lots of this is training. We have spent £10 million in the last few years on quality. We got this back, but it was an act of faith. The BS5750 (the British standard for Total Quality Management) audit is scary. We're just doing the personnel department at the moment. Total Quality means we have to look carefully at the nitty gritty of what we are about and particularly the following items:

- which folk are responsible for each task
- identify each task clearly
- write down how things are done
- list what is the training programme
- ensure that these things are always done.

The discipline of this is that it is a continuous process. This leads to new developments and initiatives because we have some energy left, as all our work is appropriate.'

Looking through the eight principles and the needs of TQM audits, there are clear areas where a competency approach would be appropriate. For example, specifying the jobs clearly and then assessing the performance of those doing the job could be competency based. Training and developing people could also be competency based. The competency approach is another piece in the puzzle of a systematic approach to management. It is a tool to use along with strategic management, human resource management and total quality management, when it comes to the business of specifying the attributes required from individual employees to make the whole thing work.

For believers, it is just a matter of time, clever analysis and sufficient resources before the system succeeds. Non-believers feel that organisations are never quite this mechanistic and the human imagination will always make greater leaps than any planned activity. The difference between these two groups seems to be reducing as the lists of competencies include more soft attributes. Certainly there is, increasingly, a move away from the earlier lists of assessable, job-specific skills to more sophisticated sets of core competencies. For example, Pickard (1993) in a study of the core competencies for staff dealing with queries from the public for South West Electricity Board had the following headings

Thoroughness
Critical thinking
Strategic thinking
Flexibility
Concern for impact
Sensitivity to the customer
Clarity of communication
Quality orientation

It could be that you want to get involved with competencies to add to the other systematic management approaches already in place in your organisation. It may be that you see competencies as a way into more systematic human resource management. If the latter, you have a much larger job to do as you work out what the basic relationships are between different initiatives and structures. This will take more time than those who are using competencies as an additional tool in an already systematic organisation.

Why should organisations get involved with competencies?

What incentives are there for organisations to get involved with competencies? There are three main areas:

1. It is one way of continuing a systematic approach to management through to what the people do at work. It focuses on what people can actually *do*.
2. There are financial and PR incentives for some organisations to become involved with national schemes which have attached 'hallmarks', for example, Investors in People and BS5750.
3. This is a slightly different sort of incentive, currently only given in countries other than the UK. States which support this concept offer real incentives for training, for instance, through their tax policies, and employment and company laws which encourage a bias towards training. In the UK there is a move in this direction by allowing personal tax allowance for NVQ courses.

On the other hand, what are the disincentives to organisations to get involved? Organisations are unlikely to get involved with NVQs where well established professional bodies are already regulating the various levels of professional competency, such as in engineering.

As an example of how difficult it is, and how long it takes to move towards competencies, a professor of electrical engineering listed the constraints they had faced in developing their job-orientated competency-based Master of Engineering course which had taken a few years to set up.

- Cost — persuading industrial companies to buy the bits for projects.
- Staffing — you need very good staff, who are very enthusiastic teachers, to run these sorts of course.
- Inertia — universities do not readily introduce fundamental change.
- Time — immovable dates of qualifying, preparing for examinations.
- Labour — students do not have previous work experience so that what is feasible is limited.
- Industry — companies need to cooperate and realise their responsibility for training in vacations, plus supervision and assessment during these vacations.

Similar constraints would exist for other organisations introducing competencies – particularly the resource issues of staff, time and money, and that of inertia would need to be dealt with. These issues must be managed and are discussed in more detail in Chapter 9.

Why do you want to measure competencies?

Answering the central question of this chapter is critical to getting going. If you are going to involve yourself in an analysis of the core competencies of the whole organisation and the strategic planning processes involved, you will need the passionate involvement of top management, and a lot of resources and time. If, on the other hand, you think it would help to identify the training needs in one department, you will need the commitment of the individuals in that department and some time to get going. Getting a feel for the scale of the undertaking is your starting point. Perhaps the most useful question to ask is, 'How much do I need this analysis?'

References

KANTER, R. M. (1989) *When Giants Learn to Dance*, Simon & Schuster, London

KAY, J. (1993) *Foundations of Corporate Success: How Business Strategies Add Value*, Oxford University Press, Oxford

LINDBLOM, C. E. (1959) The Science of Muddling Through *Public Administration Review*, American Society for Public Administration Vol 19, Spring, 79–88

LOWENDAHL, B. R. (1993) *Strategic Management of Professional Business Service Firms: Three Generic Strategies* (unpublished paper). The Norwegian School of Management, PO Box 580, 1301 Sandvika, Norway

MINTZBERG, H., QUINN, J. B. and JAMES, R. M. (1988) *The Strategy Process – Concepts, Contexts and Cases*, Prentice Hall, Englewood Cliffs, New Jersey

MOORE, J. I. (1992) *Writers on Strategy and Strategic Management*, Penguin, Harmondsworth

MORGAN, G. (1986) *Images of Organization*, Sage Publications, Beverley Hills, Calif.

PETERS, T. and AUSTIN, N. (1985) *A Passion for Excellence: The Leadership Difference*, Random House, New York

PICKARD, J. (1993) Switching to Core Skills *Personnel Management*, Nov., 60–61

PORTER, M. E. (1980) *Competitive Strategy: Techniques for Analyzing Industries and Competitors*, The Free Press, New York

PORTER, M. E. (1985) *Competitive Advantage: Creating and Sustaining Superior Performance*, The Free Press, New York

PRAHALAD, C. K. and HAMEL, G. (1990) The Core Competence of the Corporation *Harvard Business Review*, May–June, 79–91

QUINN, J. E. (1980) *Strategies for Change: Logical Incrementalism*, Richard D. Irwin, Homewood, Illinois

STALK, G., EVANS, P. and SHULMAN, L. E. (1992) Competing on Capabilities: The New Rules of Corporate Strategy *Harvard Business Review*, March–April, 57–69

STOREY, J. (1992) HRM in Action: The Truth Is Out at Last *Personnel Management*, April, 28–31

THOMPSON, A. A. and STRICKLAND, A. J. (1990) *Strategic Management: Concept and Cases*, Richard D. Irwin, Homewood, Illinois

4

Do I Want to Use Competencies for a Specific Purpose?

Chapter 3 was about introducing competencies on a grand scale. Not everyone either wants, or has the opportunity, to do this. It may be you want to use competencies to deal with an identified need. Alternatively, you might want to try using a competency approach on a small scale, to see how it goes and develop your competency in using the approach, before tackling a larger part of the organisation. It is quite likely that the resources available to you in terms of time, people and 'clout' are such that a smaller scale approach is feasible whereas an organisation-wide project would need the commitment of top management and require you to present a formal case. For many it is most appropriate to start using a competency approach in the area they are responsible for, which may or may not lead on to grander things. This chapter deals with some areas where specific projects using competencies are likely to occur. These are human resource planning, recruitment, appraisal, training, and external pressures.

These are mostly traditional personnel and HRM subjects. The use of a competency approach to these is really making them more systematic and focused rather than being fundamentally different. Where an organisation already has fairly sophisticated HRM policies and procedures in place the move to using competencies is not a very big one. A competency approach focuses on performance and must be related to the performances needed to do the appropriate work to get the business. We still need things like human resource planning, recruitment, appraisal and training but, instead of rather vague guesses as to what we want, we can now specify more particularly what is needed. Using competencies as the basis of these personnel procedures can help to make them more systematic and orientated to what we want people to do. This concentration on the behaviours, performance and specific attributes helps to keep the business of the organisation at the centre of the decisions about such things as human resource planning, recruitment, appraisal and training. This chapter looks at some of the main HRM and personnel procedures which could be done using a competency approach. Any of them may be your starting point for getting involved with competencies.

Human resource planning

Every organisation needs to have some idea about what sort, and how many, people they are going to need in the future. This process is called human resource or manpower planning. A feature of this sort of activity has been the use of job analysis and skills analysis. To change to using competency analysis is not fundamental but would permit linking in with other developments later on.

Questions to ask yourself

Is there some new project planned?

How many and what sort of people will be needed to do the work?

Who is getting near to retirement age and how will we be able to replace their expertise?

Do we need to start training someone up now?

What is the age range in our department, unit or organisation?

Does this mean in ten years' time there will be too many chiefs?

Will we all have retired?

Will the current plans for investment in new machinery mean we need less people in the future?
If so how are we going to manage the reduction?

Do we need to improve our utilisation of people by looking at job efficiency, productivity and staffing levels?

Do we need to improve our employment policies in relation to pay and benefits, training or recruitment?

Have we got a long-term problem that we can start working on now?

These questions, and many others, are put together with the future plans of the organisation and a human resource plan is developed.

The main objective of human resource planning is to interpret the company's forecasts, such as production and sales, in terms of human resource requirements. Another objective is to indicate what human resource constraints there may be on company policy in the future; for example, shortage of trained personnel, new local employer, changes in the rules applicable to part-time employees. Human resource planning is normally a specialist's task, undertaken within the personnel function, but it would involve the following processes:

1. It would be necessary to convert the plans, objectives and commitments of the organisation into human requirements.
2. Detailed information about the current employees needs to be collected. This includes ages, jobs, training and turnover.
3. An analysis of the possible supply of people from outside is useful.

The plan will require frequent adaptation as things change but will be the main, central reference point for decisions about recruiting and selecting staff. This involves decisions about both newcomers to the organisation and new jobs for established staff.

One way of approaching HR planning is to make it competency based by analysing what competencies are required and matching these with what is available within the organisation through training and development and by recruitment. This may be your starting point for getting involved with competencies.

The systematic approach to recruitment

Recruiting people for an organisation means understanding what sort of person we want for the job and then assessing the candidates who are available for selection. These have both involved various forms of behavioural and functional analysis in the past and a change to using competency analysis is, again, not fundamental.

A recruitment system must be capable of producing enough suitable candidates, cost-effective and fair. ACAS (1986) have an excellent, free, booklet to help with the whole process of recruitment and selection.

Questions to ask yourself when a vacancy occurs

Do we want the same job to be done or have there been changes?

Do we anticipate any changes in this job in the foreseeable future?

Are we going to reorganise the work of this section soon?

When these questions have been answered, the next step is to write a job description which describes the work and responsibilities of the job. ACAS suggest that a good job description can be made if the following points are remembered:

Main purpose of job – try to describe this in one sentence; if you cannot find a main purpose, perhaps the whole job needs reviewing.

Main tasks of the job – always use active verbs, like 'writing', 'filing', 'milling', 'repairing', to describe precisely what is done, rather than vague terms such as 'in charge of', 'deals with'.

Scope of the job – although the 'main tasks' describe what is done, they don't necessarily indicate the scope or importance of the job. This can be done by describing the value of equipment or materials handled, the degree of precision required, and the number of people supervised, etc.

ACAS (1986), p. 4

You might also want to list the main duties of the job holder. One approach to writing the job description is to describe the competencies required for someone to do the job. The job description not only helps with the recruitment but can also suggest ways of inducting and training the newcomer.

Once you have a job description, it is then possible to draw up a person specification. This describes the knowledge, skills and abilities that an ideal candidate would have. Two well-established classifications exist to help this process: Rodger's (1952) Seven-Point Plan and Fraser's (1950) Five-Fold Grading System.

Another option is to use competencies. The important thing is to set appropriate levels for the characteristics for the particular job. Too high a specification may produce no suitable candidates, too low a specification may underestimate the problems associated with the job being done badly.

Selection techniques

The complexity of the job to be filled will be reflected in the nature of the selection process. For a straightforward job, a short interview and perhaps a simple test may be all that is required. For other, more complex jobs a more varied strategy may be required. Some of the traditional methods are listed in Figure 4.1 but for further detail, see Plumbley (1991). It is important, whichever methods are used, that the immediate supervisor is involved in the selection decision to ensure that they are committed to welcoming the new worker. Similarly, the candidate will have the opportunity of assessing whether they can work for the supervisor. The selection can become competency based, for example in an assessment centre favoured for management selection. Details on how to do the assessment based on competencies are given in Chapter 7.

Figure 4.1
Traditional selection methods

Selection tests – tests of attainments and typical performances related to the skills necessary to do the job

Group selection – developed to assess the candidate's ability to get on with and influence other people

Psychological tests – can be tests of general intelligence, special aptitudes, motivation, attitudes or personality

References – frequently used in the public sector

The interview – an essential part of the ritual of getting to know each other

From appraisal to performance management

Another time when assessing individuals at work occurs, and so using competency-based analysis may be considered, is for appraisal purposes. Performance appraisal is intended to provide milestones, feedback, guidance and monitoring. A further development is tying it into a larger and more complete system of performance management. These systems, which are increasingly being used (see for example, Fowler, 1988), highlight appraisal as a central activity in the good management of staff. The difference from traditional appraisal is that the assessment process tends to be more rigorous and objective, and is clearly linked into precise job definitions and organisational objective setting, individual development plans and the pay system. A competency-based approach to these developments would be most appropriate and you may be thinking of doing this.

Questions to ask yourself

Why do managers seek to appraise the performance of organisation members?
- For social control?
- To meet human resource considerations?
- To identify the development and training that individuals need?
- To aid the decision making involved in determining who goes where in career developments?
- Preparing for future manpower requirements?
- Managing performance?

The increased interest in systematic management in the last ten years has led to the development of performance management. There has been an emphasis on specifying what is wanted and rewarding individuals. The normal stages of performance management are:

1. Written and agreed job descriptions, reviewed regularly. Objectives for the work group which have been cascaded down from the organisation's strategic objectives.
2. Individual objectives derived from the above, which are jointly devised by appraiser and appraisee. These objectives

are results rather than task oriented, are tightly defined and include measures to be assessed. The objectives are designed to stretch the individual, and offer potential development as well as meeting business needs.

3. Development plan, devised by manager and individual, detailing development goals and activities designed to enable the individual to meet their objectives. These could be competency based. The emphasis here is on managerial support and coaching.

4. Assessment of objectives. Ongoing formal reviews on a regular basis designed to motivate the appraisee and concentrate on developmental issues. This could be competency based. Also there is usually an annual assessment which affects pay received, depending on performance in achievement of objectives.

One of the major advantages of performance management is managers are forced to give emphasis to formal and planned employee development, indeed a similar system described by Harper (1988) is referred to as 'Performance Review and Development'). Another advantage is that it also enforces a clear role description and set of objectives agreed by managers and individuals. On the down side, there is potential conflict between the aim of improving job performance, which requires openness and a developmental approach, and the link with pay. This conflict is resolved by separating the performance development and the performance pay reviews and holding them at different times of the year.

The essential elements of appraisal are *judgement and reporting*. The performance is not simply being measured, as in the completion of a work quota, it is being judged. This obviously involves discretion, worry about bias and the possibility of being quite wrong. This judgement not only has to be made, but also passed on to other people in such a way that the other(s) understand what is intended and take action on it. Those devising performance appraisal schemes devote most of their energies to finding ways of making the judgements as systematic as possible and the reporting as consistent as possible between different appraisers. One of the ways of trying to be more systematic is to use a competency-based approach, but even then a judgement about whether the person is competent has to be made.

Much of what has been written about the appraisal process concentrates on the personal interaction. George (1986) suggests that an effective appraisal scheme is dependent on the style and content of appraisal not conflicting with the culture of the organisation. He suggests that the degree of openness that is required in the appraisal process is:

'unlikely to materialise without an atmosphere of mutual trust and respect – something which is conspicuously lacking in many employing organisations.'

George (1986) p. 32

The appraisal, therefore, needs to reflect the wider values of the organisation in order for it to be properly integrated into the organisation and to survive in an effective form. The appraisal system can, in fact, be used to display and support the culture and style of the organisation. George suggests that it can be used to help integrate people into an explicit and purposeful culture. The appraisal process may also be used to help *change* the culture in an organisation, but this would need to be done in conjunction with other supportive activities and be seen to be led from the top. If appraisal is used in this way, it may be a way into taking a systematic approach to core competencies in an organisation.

Training

Often the first people to use a competency approach within an organisation are the training people. There has been an enormous increase in interest in training within organisations over the last ten years. This is due, in part, to national pressure, as was discussed in Chapter 2. Despite the sometimes religious fervour of people working in training, the results have not, so far, always been as widespread as was hoped. Reid et al. (1992, p. 51) suggest that, on the whole, training in British industry can best be described as peripheral. I have based the following questions on their findings.

Questions to ask yourself

What operational priority does training have?

Is training in your organisation integrated with the mainstream operations?

Does training normally appear among strategic plans?

Is it a peripheral activity for most line management?

Does training usually function via *ad hoc*, unrelated events?

Is training mentioned as part of new capital projects, product launches, reorganisation plans, etc?

Does training count as an expense or an investment?

With all the national pressure to get involved with training (see Chapter 2), what is in it for organisations? Why should they spend time, effort and money on training? As long ago as 1982, before the main drive for training, Tyson and York gave a useful list:

1. Maximising productivity and output.
2. Developing the versatility and employability of human resources.
3. Developing the cohesiveness of the whole organisation and its sub-groups.
4. Increasing job satisfaction, motivation and morale.
5. Developing a consciousness of the importance of safety at work and improving standards.
6. Making the best use of available material, resources, equipment, and methods.
7. Standardising organisational practices and procedures.

Tyson and York (1982), p. 178

Any or all of these may concern a specific department, manager or job holder at any particular time. The training personnel in large organisations will be concerned with trying to integrate these into the overall policies of the organisation. This is a time-consuming job and takes longer to achieve than many expect.

The current development of human resource management (HRM) in the personnel field tries to integrate training and development with a whole range of other aspects of managing people in the work place (see, for example, Keep, 1989).

Deciding what to train

If we see training as the process of bringing someone to a level of competency, we have to know *what* is required. As a training objective, for instance, the manager will want the trainee to understand the task to be performed and what is required to reach a level of competency. So the manager has to decide how much understanding is needed at the outset in order to provide a satisfactory basis for the training. There are two aspects to this: assessing training needs associated with the job and assessing those associated with the individual.

Job analysis can be done in several different ways. It can be a comprehensive analysis of *all* the skills and understanding required to do a job, that is the competencies necessary for the job. This would involve a detailed study of everything involved over a full cycle of the job. Alternatively, it may be appropriate to look at a part of the job where there are problems, or which is critical to performance of the job, or where new approaches are needed. More detailed explanations of these methods are given in Chapter 6 and can be found in specialised books (see for example, Reid et al., 1992). This analysis leads to a job specification which gives details of the mental and physical activities, or competencies, of the job and the environment where the job is done. The skills and knowledge, or competencies, required to do these are then listed.

Individual analysis, which is the assessment of a person's competency at doing the tasks, can also be done in several ways. It might include self analysis or assessment centres, where experts evaluate performance on set tasks. The most usual way, however, is as part of the performance appraisal process described earlier. This might involve systematic observations of the individual at work, collecting evidence of their performance, or the informal understanding reached by daily working together – some of these are described in Chapter 7.

A comparison can then be made between the job analysis and the individual analysis and any differences will lead to a diagnosis of training needs – the so-called training gap. It may be that new techniques are being introduced, it may be that old skills have faded or that there has never been sufficient understanding to do the job to optimum level.

A systematic approach to training is well suited to using a competency methodology to analyse and identify training needs, and has been well received by trainers. This systematic approach is now widely accepted in training departments. However, it should always be remembered that the whole process is dependent on judgement at various points and so, appropriately, should also involve managers from outside the training department.

External influences

So far we have discussed reasons for choosing a competency approach because it will help the organisation on either a grand scale or in some smaller way. But people also get involved with competencies because they have been persuaded by others to do so. Sometimes the response is a cynical one to an order to generate lists of competency from a senior who wishes to be 'seen' to be doing this, or because some outside agency promises some support if the lists are generated. Sometimes it is a response to outside pressure, such as from TEED or the TECs (see Chapter 2). At times, it may be a straightforward response, 'being prepared to give it a go' because it seems a good idea; or it is seen as a way of funding a project or keeping something going which could not have been done otherwise. People will go along with using competencies as a vehicle to get what they want out of the project.

Many examples can be found in education where pump-priming money was, and is, available to introduce a competency-based approach to, say, vocational skills. This has been used by the department or institution to deliver a pet project as well as the vocational competencies. In most cases everyone is happy – the pump primers get what they want, the educational institution gets what it wants and the students may well get more than they would have otherwise. There are, of course, times when the rules have been bent rather further than the fundholder hoped and these have led to increased monitoring, evaluation and report writing of schemes. Whether this is actually more cost-effective than allowing for a few stray projects is arguable, but it is certainly more accountable.

Sometimes the response to do competency-based analysis or training is prompted by outside pressure for 'hallmarked' standards, many of which are competency based. The most obvious example from the last few years has been the rise and rise of the quality standards BS5750 and ISO 9000. Many organisations have taken these on because their customers demand them as part of their own quality audit. For example, building contractors may demand this from suppliers of materials for building a bridge. Similarly many qualifications, particularly NVQ ones, are competency based. Where an employer or employee wants to conform to these, they will have to get involved with competencies.

Why should individuals get involved with competencies?

The main incentive for individuals to get involved with competencies, and particularly NVQs, would be if potential employers were interested. So what is the view from employers? We, Torrington, Weightman and Peacock (1992), asked employers what they knew of MCI and/or NVQs, and they generally replied with little enthusiasm. Perhaps things have changed since then, with so much Government money being spent to promote them. There was similar uncertainty and lack of commitment when we asked about the potential value of students collecting towards the MCI awards. A typical answer, from a large electronics company, was:

'Until more people realise what MCI is trying to achieve, it won't matter. It does address some of the areas that we find lacking from our graduates.'

We then asked whether the employers would help graduates finish collecting evidence so that they could achieve an MCI award. Half the employers said they would, if possible, and half said they would not, as they preferred their employees to follow their own in-house programmes. Another incentive for individuals to get involved with competencies would be if they became aware of their own self development through, for example, using log books. A production manager from an electricity supply company said:

> 'It is not a bad idea for anyone to keep a log book. I keep one and it is very useful. I would not think any more of a person just because they kept one, it is how they perform that matters. It is no good to an employer; it is only for personal benefit. If they keep a log book against certain criteria, if they have to prove their ability, it shows they can perform.'

Another motivator is that competency-based qualifications allow those with unconventional experience to have their expertise acknowledged. The Government argue that NVQs and professional qualifications also allow greater mobility for individuals. They become less dependent on the particular employer who recognises their competency. In-house, non-qualification-based competency assessment and training will help individuals to develop competencies which enhance their employability within the organisation and outside.

On the other hand, what disincentives are there for individuals? First, it can be very time consuming trying to collect all the evidence for the formal national assessment procedures. Second, the way in which competency approaches are handled can be very influential. For instance, if competencies are used very mechanistically and specifically individuals can feel over-controlled and stifled.

References

ACAS (1986) *Recruitment and Selection*, Advisory Booklet No 6, Advisory Conciliation and Arbitration Service

FOWLER, A. (1988) New Directions in Performance Pay *Personnel Management*, 30–4

Fraser, J. M. (1950) *Employment Interviewing*, Macdonald & Evans, London

GEORGE, J. (1986) Appraisal in the Public Sector: Dispensing with the Big Stick *Personnel Management*, May, 32–5

HARPER, S. C. (1988) A Developmental Approach to Performance appraisal *Business Horizons*, Sept/Oct, 158–74

KEEP, E. (1989) A Training Scandal? *Personnel Management in Britain* (ed. K. Sisson), Blackwell, Oxford

PLUMBLEY, P. (1991) *Recruitment and Selection*, 5th edn, IPM, London

REID, M. A., BARRINGTON, H. and KENNEY, J. (1992) *Training Interventions; Managing Employee Development*, 3rd ed:, IPM, London

RODGER, A. (1952) *The Seven-Point Plan*, National Institute of Industrial Psychology, London

TORRINGTON, D., WEIGHTMAN, J. and PEACOCK, A. (1992) MCI Competence Standards and Engineering and Science Students at UMIST. Unpublished report for TEED, July

TYSON, S. and YORK, A. (1982) *Personnel Management Made Simple*, Heinemann, London

5

What Sort of Competencies Do I Want?

Is the purpose of developing people in the organisation to improve the understanding of basic principles, assist the acquisition of skills, or to impart fact-based knowledge? Often the response is 'yes' to them all. For example, the management training and development officer from an electricity supply company summed up this whole dilemma:

> 'They have to be good engineers and good managers. We need technically competent individuals who can make decisions about how to get the electricity back on.'

This means understanding basic principles of electricity supply and developing general competencies about managing to get things done.

On the other hand, there are some who want to use competencies to raise the minimum level. An MCI coordinator said to us:

> 'MCI is not about the top 10 per cent but about getting the ordinary standard up. We want undergraduates to understand about continuous development.'

Deciding what sort of competency to list, assess and develop will depend on the ideology, purpose and passions of those responsible. Some of the heated debate within the field of NVQs and among trainers is because people are trying to do different things. Some organisations have resolved this dilemma by using the term 'competencies' to refer only to generalised, transferable competencies and reserving the terms 'skills' and 'knowledge' for the technical aspects of jobs.

This chapter examines some of the main issues associated with deciding which sort of competencies to use for your particular purposes. There are no right answers but there are some questions which you need to consider before going ahead with your competency-based analysis.

Inputs and outputs

Questions to ask yourself

What sort of competency do we want?

Do we want to concentrate on the behaviours that lead to success?

What about personal qualities?

Do we want a list of *everything* that makes up a competent performance?

Should we list the obvious – is it obvious to everyone?

Do I know what each of the listed competencies means?

What counts as a competency?

What does someone have to do to achieve this competency?

One of the main issues in discussing competency is about whether the analysis is over *inputs* or *outputs*. That is, should the analysis concentrate on the elements which go to producing the appropriate performance or should the competencies be seen as the appropriate performance? Debate on this can reach theological proportions but the central issue of whether to concentrate on the inputs or outputs does affect what the competencies will be and, consequently, what training, assessment and so on will take place.

For example, when I worked with metally handicapped children in the early 1970s we often wanted to teach children to feed themselves with a spoon, that is, to be competent at spoon-feeding. One approach was to look at the sequence of behaviour displayed by normal children learning to do this and teach the mentally handicapped using this observed developmental pathway. So we might teach such things as eating with hands, banging the spoon on the dish, helping to carry the filled spoon to the mouth, and so on. This method concentrated on the *inputs* to the child to ensure the natural developmental connections were established. The other approach was to analyse the task of spoon-feeding into its component parts, breaking these down into suitably small behaviours to teach. So using behaviour modification techniques of clear instructions and rewards to ensure systematic teaching, we taught such things as holding the spoon, moving the spoon to the mouth, opening the mouth, and swallowing. Here we were concentrating on the *outputs*, so the final behaviour was the desired competency. Being pragmatists, we found that both sorts of teaching were required as the input approach could take forever while the output approach could not be achieved without some of the natural developmental sequence being in place. Even with one-to-one teaching, we could not possibly teach everything on a behaviour modification schedule so had to depend on inputs leading to competency in some areas.

An example from work might be whether to concentrate on the underlying personal characteristics which lead to good salespeople, i.e. inputs, or to specify the detailed required behaviours we consider make good salespeople, i.e. outputs.

An input approach concentrates on what characteristics distinguish a superior performance. For example, managers might have a mixture of aptitudes, attitudes and personal attributes as the basis of their being seen as an effective manager. So, to develop a generalised list of competencies, a higher order list of inputs which can handle individual variation is reasonable (see the Boyatzis 1982 study of 2000 American managers).

The outcome approach is dominated by the ability to perform at work – the ability to achieve. Then functional analysis is done to find out what you need to do to achieve the performance. The NVQ standards use this approach with an emphasis on analysis of the key purpose of the job. When the key purpose is agreed, you ask what needs to happen for it to be achieved. This last question is asked again and again, to break each step down further. Decisions about when to stop the analysis will be taken on the basis of who you are looking at and the level at which they are working.

This debate about concentrating on inputs or outputs is current in the competency movement; this is not just a rarefied academic discussion. Depending which conclusion one makes, determines how one looks at the staff of the organisation. If one concentrates on outputs, a systematic analysis of the job required is necessary and then individuals are recruited and trained to this specification. If the input approach is taken, then again a systematic analysis of the job is done but the personal qualities of people able to do these well are assessed, which may also include the ability to do other things as well.

Frequently the term 'competency' is used for the input approach and 'competence' for the output approach (see for example, Reid et al., 1992). It may be that the two approaches are useful for different purposes. Where a straightforward task is needed, an outcomes analysis may be useful. But for a more complex job with unpredictable aspects in the future, perhaps the personal qualities associated with inputs may prove more useful. As an example, selection for a computer programmer for a six-month contract is likely to concentrate on outputs, whereas selecting someone to develop the use of computing over the next five years might take an inputs approach.

Size of chunks

One issue that leads to endless discussion and will never be concluded to everyone's satisfaction is what size chunks of behaviour to include in the list of competencies. If the statements are too large and general they are non-discriminating; if they are too small and detailed they are irritating, prescriptive and controlling. It is a nice judgement what size to have. For example, in our (Weightman, Blandamer and Torrington 1991) lists of personnel professional competencies for the NHS (mentioned at the end of Chapter 1), we had such things as appraisal/assessment, attendance management and management of poor performance included in the overall role of performance monitor. We could have had just the roles. Equally well, we could have broken down appraisal/assessment in more detail – the ability to design and explain an appraisal process; provide appropriate training and materials for appraisers; the ability to communicate the need for appraisal and assessment to employees; the ability to engender the employee's commitment to the process; and so on. We included these later, for referral, as we felt they would have been very frustrating and unwieldly in the main document. We could, indeed, then have specified the competencies which go to allow someone to do each item on the detailed list – such as what comprises an ability to design and explain an appraisal process. This can go on for ever. Knowing when it is appropriate to stop is the clever thing; no one will use a metre-high document!

The advantages of prescribing competencies in detail are it imposes order, which, in turn, can lead to better coordination between jobs, less duplication of effort and allow resources to be allocated on a rational basis. Detailed lists are particularly useful where there is a shortage of competent staff or where there are a lot of temporary or inexperienced staff. Highly specific lists are also useful where there is a high turnover of staff. One example of this is the McDonald's hamburger chain who have shown that their detailed lists of competencies for each stage of the operation can enable young students to produce a consistent product all over the world.

There are, however, serious disadvantages to detailed competency lists: they can lead to minimum contribution from staff, 'working to rule' and inflexibility. Overprescription generates no enthusiasm, excitement or creativity. If things are prescribed too precisely, we feel over-controlled and start resenting the control. The whole point of the empowerment movement in organisations has been to encourage individuals to show initiative and take responsibility (see Block, 1987; Kanter, 1989). If these individuals then have very tight competency assessments of how they get things done, they will not feel empowered. Prescription has become something of the new orthodoxy in management, with attempts to prescribe everything – from the BS5750 quality procedures to competencies. Some of this is in the vain hope that the world can be made more stable by procedures and systems.

Yet again, it is the balance that matters; in this case between describing the right competencies without overprescribing for the particular environment. Which parts of management should be tightly controlled and which loosely held to allow development is a continuing fascination of management and is well discussed in more general texts on management. Equally, which competencies it is useful to specify tightly and which to leave loose has become an art in using competencies effectively.

One way round this is to have competencies listed in reasonably large chunks but then to break these down into smaller chunks when the need arises. For example, if someone is assessed as not competent in the area then a closer analysis of which bit is not fully developed can be assessed and compensated for. In our personnel example, only when there was a felt need would people move from the general listing to the more detailed lists, and then on to specific training and development materials which were listed and gave even more detailed analysis of the competencies involved.

General or specific competencies?

Similar to the size of chunk debate is the issue about whether to have lists of general or specific competencies.

Questions to ask yourself

What do we want to count as a competency?

Should it include technical knowledge?

How do we ensure we don't get bogged down in the obvious?

Are there generic competencies common to groups of staff as well as specific ones?

The specific competencies associated with particular jobs may include technical skills and knowledge. They may also include particular ways of behaving. In most organisations these are separated from a general list of transferable behaviours which are called general competencies and cover such areas as communication, working with others, vision and creativity. The difficulty is that these are seen as being required by most people working in the organisation, but in different ways.

Different levels of competency

The answer to this issue may include having general competencies listed at different levels for jobs at different places in the hierarchy. The level of competency in each of the elements to be assessed needs to be clarified.

Figure 5.1
Communication and representational skills: examples of competencies required at different levels of seniority

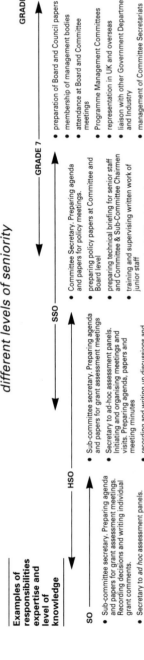

Examples of responsibilities expertise and level of knowledge

SO ——— HSO ——— SSO ——— GRADE 7 ——— GRADE 6

SO
- Sub-committee secretary. Preparing agenda and papers for grant assessment meetings. Recording decisions and writing individual grant comments.
- Secretary to *ad hoc* assessment panels. Organising meetings and visits. Drafting minutes of meetings. Preparing agenda and papers.
- briefing – oral and written for Sub-committee Chairmen.
- drafting technical briefings for senior staff
- communication of policy and regulations to the academic and industrial community.
- familiarity with computer graphics for presentations

HSO
- Sub-committee secretary. Preparing agenda and papers for grant assessment meetings
- Secretary to *ad hoc* assessment panels. Initiating and organising meetings and visits. Preparing agenda, papers and meeting minutes
- recording and writing up discussions and decisions on grant application
- oral and written briefing for Committee and Sub-committee Chairmen
- preparing technical briefing for senior staff
- communication of policy and regulations to academia and industry
- drafting of Committee policy papers
- drafting of grant recommendations for Board
- secretariat representation at meetings and peer review visits
- presentation of Committee policy to HEI departments
- commissioning and drafting publicity material
- Secretary of Committee Panel

SSO
- Committee Secretary. Preparing agenda and papers for policy meetings.
- preparing policy papers at Committee and Board level
- preparing technical briefing for senior staff and Committee & Sub-Committee Chairmen
- training and supervising written work of junior staff
- representation in UK and abroad as appropriate
- presentation of papers at meetings and conferences
- commissioning and preparing publicity material
- representing Division at internal meetings and being chair as member of ad hoc working group
- membership of recruitment/promotion panels
- tutoring and developing training courses
- assisting in preparation of case for new initiatives and new major facilities

GRADE 7 / GRADE 6
- preparation of Board and Council papers
- membership of management bodies
- attendance at Board and Committee meetings
- Programme Management Committees
- representation in UK and overseas
- liaison with other Government Departments and Industry
- management of Committee Secretariats
- attendance as necessary at International and National Central Facilities
- membership of external Management Committees

Training available centrally
- Letter and Report Writing
- Technical Writing for Scientists
- Writing Minutes of Meetings
- Interactive Skills
- Presentational Skills
- How to Run a Meeting
- Selection and Promotion Interviewing
- Facing the Media

Questions to ask yourself

Does the stated competency mean a minimum standard which everyone needs to attain or are there variations for different jobs?

How good do you have to be to be credited with the competency?

Is the stated competency an all or nothing event or are there degrees of competency?

One answer to these questions is to acknowledge that there are different levels of competency required at different stages of a career or in different jobs. Figure 5.1 shows the list of one sort of general competencies – communication and respresentational skills – drawn up by one section of the Civil Service for different levels of seniority. Note that they expect some degree of overlap, represented by the use of arrows at the top. Many organisations have systems of competencies where they show competencies varying depending on the level in the hierarchy. For example, the need for information technology competency is probably more sophisticated for middle ranks, where it peaks, and then the need fades for those at the top. Another, more detailed, example is from the Institution of Civil Engineers (1992) who distinguish five levels of management (see Figure 5.2).

Figure 5.2
Management competencies at different management levels

Management levels

The level of competence in the elements is dependent on particular career stages, and so these need to be defined.

The career stages adopted respect job titles that have universal usage in the industry and also indicate typical levels of responsibility so that, irrespective of sector, individuals can identify their present level and their next likely level.

The job titles and responsibilities used are as follows.

Top management

Typical job titles:	Chief executives, directors, partners, or most senior professional person in an organization or deputy in a large organization
Typical responsibilities:	Strategic management of organizations, in addition to the general management of the business plan for the current year

Senior management

Typical job titles:	Construction Manager, Associate, Divisional Director/Manager, Chief Engineer
Typical responsibilities:	Management of a major sector or function of an organization; a degree of autonomy of control reporting to top management

Middle management

Typical job titles:	Senior Project Engineer, Senior Project Manager, Senior Site Manager
Typical responsibilities:	Management of a major project or a number of concurrent projects, including overseeing the teams working on them

Supervisory management

Typical job titles:	Section Engineer, Senior Engineer, Project Engineer, Project Manager
Typical responsibilities:	Management of a small project or a small team, requiring professional and financial judgement with minimum supervision

Junior management

Typical job titles:	Engineer, Assistant Engineer, Graduate Engineer, Junior Engineer
Typical responsibilities:	Obtaining experience at the discretion of others, normally in the early stages of their career; taking key roles in teams as individuals, exercising direction of others on a project or part of a large project

---

Source: Institution of Civil Engineers, 1992

They also distinguish four levels of competency for each element of their ten key roles, or competences (see Figure 5.3).

Figure 5.3
Levels of competency applied to each element of the key roles

---

Levels of competence

There are four levels of competence. Each element of the key roles has the appropriate level ascribed at progressive stages of career development.

The levels of competence used are

A	Appreciation	Know what is meant by a term and what its purpose is
K	Knowledge	Understand in some detail the principles of the topic and how they are applied
E	Experience	Have acquired knowledge and skill
B	Ability	Be able to apply skill with satisfactory results

The indication of competence at varying career stages for each element in all the key roles produces the model competencies given in section 6 (Figure 5.4).

The model competencies accept that competence is either being obtained, kept current or being lost. These conditions are illustrated by arrows to represent progressive acquisition of competence, the level at which competence is to be sustained and that the competence is likely to regress from the initial peak and/or previous level indicated.

Source: Institution of Civil Engineers, 1992

These two distinctions are then mapped onto a form (see Figure 5.4) for each key role, to show the levels of competency required at different stages in a civil engineer's career.

Figure 5.4
Map of changing competencies for engineers

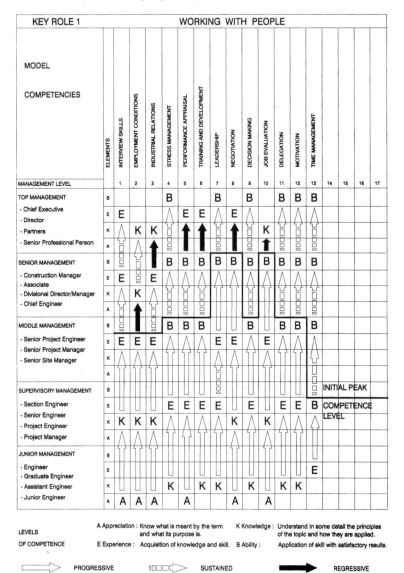

| KEY ROLE 1 | | | | WORKING WITH PEOPLE | | | | | | | | | | | | |

LEVELS OF COMPETENCE

A Appreciation : Know what is meant by the term and what its purpose is.

E Experience : Acquisition of knowledge and skill.

K Knowledge : Understand in some detail the principles of the topic and how they are applied.

B Ability : Application of skill with satisfactory results.

⇨ PROGRESSIVE   ▯▯▯⇨ SUSTAINED   ■■⯈ REGRESSIVE

Source: Institution of Civil Engineers, 1992

This model could be adapted for smaller groups – say within a work group – between beginners, job holders and experienced experts, where this distinction is useful. Equally, it could be used to show how people are expected to progress through a career and identify their own training and development needs.

Performance criteria

Related to the issue of levels is the question of what we mean by *normal* competency. Normal can mean several things. There is normal in the medical sense of working perfectly; there is normal in the average sense of at least 50 per cent work this way; there is normal in the adequate sense, in that most people would work this way. You need to consider whether your list of competencies is about perfection, average or adequate behaviours. You may decide to have different criteria for each competency. Certainly there has been much discussion about this aspect of the national standards and whether they encourage a lowest common denominator approach to competencies.

Questions to ask yourself

Do you want to have levels within each competency such as adequate, good, excellent as many appraisal schemes have?

Do you want a matrix to suggest varying levels of expertise in the different competencies associated with different jobs?

Is this becoming too elaborate?

Perhaps you will settle for just one sort of normal, but which?

Answering the questions about what you mean by normal leads on to deciding what *performance criteria* will be applied. Performance criteria are statements about how the competency will be judged. These usually consist of five or six sentences describing a range of different ways the behaviour can be demonstrated – the how, where, with whom and to what level the competency could be demonstrated to be considered as competent behaviour. For example, the Institution of Civil Engineers had a set of performance criteria, which they called a glossary of terms, for their key role 1: Working with people (see Figure 5.5).

Figure 5.5
Performance criteria applied by ICE to key role 1:
Working with people

Glossary of terms used in the elements

Key role 1: Working with people

1. *Interview skills:* Questioning and listening techniques to acquire information in order to assess capabilities and use information obtained as appropriate.

2. *Employment conditions:* Statutory or other rules under which people are employed.

3. *Industrial relations:* A framework established to avoid conflict, which reflects the fact that employees react to their work in varying ways.

4. *Stress management:* Recognizing the consequences of pressure applied to achieve results and exercising awareness, concern and control on behalf of self and others.

5. *Performance appraisal:* A procedure by which the growth and development of individuals and organizations can be monitored and communicated to mutual advantage.

6. *Training and development:* A structured approach towards enhancing the effectiveness of people in their current work, which provides for the future needs of the individuals and the organization.

7. *Leadership:* The initiative and vision that encourages others to carry out tasks under direction.

8. *Negotiation:* Planned discussion and bargaining that consistently allows acceptable agreement to be reached.

9. *Decision-making:* Judgement exercised with responsibility once all relevant factors have been taken into account.

10. *Job evaluation:* The determination of skills required to carry out specific tasks or functions.

11. *Delegation:* The act of giving responsibility and authority for a function or task to another while remaining accountable.

12. *Motivation:* Selection of the appropriate technique with which to generate enthusiasm in self and others to produce the best performance in their duties.

13. *Time management:* The establishment of priorities that ensures objectives are met, fully recognizing time as a resource.

Source: Institution of Civil Engineers, 1992

70

The criteria may well include a description of what sorts of evidence of this performance will be accepted, particularly for NVQs. Where the performance criteria include qualitative words such as 'appropriate', 'adequate' and 'relevant' there will also need to be some indication of the range of behaviours that are considered competent for the list.

For internal use within an organisation setting, the performance criteria and range statements are often most usefully set and drafted by the people who actually do the jobs. In a large chemical company, each section selected their own competency list from a central common list and then set appropriate performance criteria for the section. Similarly, nurses on the ward are involved in setting 'nursing standards' that are competency based.

A refinement of this approach is to then put in statements about the range of behaviour which is acceptable for the particular competency to be credited. The major problem with these is the whole document can become too large and unwieldy, and consequently very difficult for people to use. This has certainly been a major criticism of some of the NVQ lead bodies' materials, where the assessment procedure can only be operated by professional competency people. Where the judgement is not critical and to be 'set in stone', it seems better to try to keep things as simple as possible.

Sampling

The validity of the list of competencies can be affected by the sample of those studied. Sampling is an issue which concerns researchers enormously but it is worth considering at a practical level as the results can be biased by including people who are not really part of the population or not representative of the population as a whole. For example, studying only the very best performer and then judging everyone else by this standard is unlikely to be seen as either equitable or achievable by the majority.

Sampling means deciding which example of time, place, activity, behaviour should be looked at to arrive at a representative picture of a whole population. In most cases the sampling for competency assessment is obvious to everyone, as the particular competency is easily observed in the general run of things, or is only likely to happen at particular times. The use of sampling is worth considering where only a brief assessment period is available. In this case, it may be necessary to take formal decisions to make observations at random or predetermined times. Questions about how representative the period of observation or assessment is need to be asked. It may actually be better to ask how *unusual* it was, as few people admit to having a 'typical' day. The real question is, have you missed any vital evidence? It is usually worth asking the job holder's opinion and, if they feel aggrieved, some further assessment may be called for. As usual a cost-effective approach has to be taken; it makes no sense for an organisation to spend all its time assessing and monitoring when they have a business to run.

There are three main issues to consider when deciding on the sample size. Work and expense increase as the sample size increases. Each extra member has less impact than the previous one. However, the credibility, or face validity, of the scheme depends on having a reasonably sized sample.

Reliability and validity

These are two technical terms used about assessment procedures generally. All attempts to make judgements more systematic and objective are attempts to make them more reliable and valid.

Questions to ask yourself

Is this assessment measuring the right things?

Is the assessment specific enough?

How can I make the assessment more reliable?

Is the assessment valid?

Reliability means that the measurement measures the same or a similar thing every time. It is an attempt to deal with the following sorts of questions. If I use this method today, will I get similar results if I use it tomorrow? For example, does a particular exercise in an assessment centre measure similar competencies when I use it in April as it would in September? Would you get similar results if it was done by different people?

Validity is another technical consideration. The term means that the measurement actually measures what it was intended to. For example, is an assessment centre based on competencies a valid measurement of the management behaviour of candidates? There are several sorts of validity?

- *Face validity* means that it looks like a suitable or appropriate measure. This is important for getting people to go along with the measurement and the results. For example, if you are going to assess my competence for a management post, some assessment involving my ability to influence people is likely to have higher face validity than if you assess my ability to play golf.
- *Concurrent validity* means that similar measures arrive at a similar result. For example, if we were testing a new selection procedure involving testing for competencies, we might see if we get concurrent results with a measure we have relied on in the past.
- *Predictive validity* is about the ability of the measure to predict outcomes. Taking our competency-based selection device, we would need to follow up the results to see if our new assessment device was selecting better than previous methods. Pragmatically, the validity of any approach is governed by its utility as a predictor of behaviours rather than in setting artificially precise standards.

Two other technical terms in use in the assessing of competencies are *validation* and *verification*. Validation and verification are words used particularly in conjunction with NVQ competencies. Validation is a complex business but essentially means that some process of ensuring validity of the process has been attempted. Verification is also a complex business but means checking up that what has been claimed really has taken place. So, for example, if you were showing me a log book of your activities to claim a degree of competency against the MCI standards, validation would be ensuring that the log book was an appropriate device for demonstrating these competencies and verification would mean my checking that you really had done these things and had benefited from the experience.

The job composite model of competencies

As an example of how we (Torrington, Waite and Weightman, 1992) tried to overcome some of these problems, there follows a more detailed description of the case, first discussed in Chapter 1, of personnel workers in a regional health service.

Our analysis started by considering not whether a *person* is able to do a specific job, but what *skills* are required in order to be able to do that job – the approach of output competency analysis. This led to the professional competencies. We then analysed the personal attributes of those who managed to get the job done effectively – input competency analysis. This led to the generic competencies. Figure 5.6 summarises the main areas of expertise or professional competence that are comprehended by each professional role. There is also a list of generic competencies which are more general competencies used in at least two, and sometimes more, of the professional roles.

The idea of the job composite model, therefore, is that each individual's job will be a composite of activities drawn from the professional list and from the shorter list of generic competencies. Job specific, individual training needs can then be derived by using our self-assessment questionnaire, which is a more detailed version of Figure 5.6.

To help explain how this works, here are two hypothetical examples – for a pay strategy post and a recruitment officer – of the sort of competencies, both professional and generic, that particular job holders might conclude were necessary for them to do their work. These lists may be arrived at by the job holder alone or in consultation with their boss and/or colleagues.

Figure 5.6
Job composite model of competencies: an example of self-assessment questionnaire

Name .... Date....................................

Current post ....

Using the job composite model of personnel competencies, complete the following checklist by assessing your present expertise in each of the identified competencies as either A, B, C, D or E, indicating:

A   Little or no expertise;

B   Some expertise, but a need for further development or updating now;

C   Expert;

D   Considerable expertise, but some further development or updating necessary soon;

E   Not relevant to the present post.

Professional competences

1. The PM as selector

.... Vacancy identification
.... Job analysis
.... Recruitment advertising
.... Selection process
.... Psychometric testing
.... Selection decision making
.... Letters of offer
.... Contracts of employment
.... Employee records
.... Induction/socialization

2. The PM as paymaster

.... Job evaluation
.... Pay determination
.... Employee benefits
.... Performance related pay
.... Salary administration
.... Salary structures
.... Pensions and sick pay
.... Taxation and National Insurance

3. The PM as negotiator

.... Consultation
.... Employee involvement
.... Negotiating bodies
.... Trade union recognition
.... Agreements and procedures
.... Grievance and discipline
.... Redundancy and dismissal
.... Industrial tribunals

4. The PM as performance monitor

.... Appraisal/assessment
.... Attendance management
.... Management of poor performance

5. The PM as welfare officer

.... Health and safety
.... Counselling services
.... Occupational health
.... Health and safety legislation

6. The PM as human resource planner

.... Supply and demand forecasting
.... Modelling and extrapolation
.... Manpower utilization
.... Planning
.... Statistical method
.... Computer analysis

7. The PM as trainer

.... Identification of training needs
.... Design of training
.... Delivery of training
.... Evaluation of training

8. The PM as communicator

.... Bulletins
.... Community relations
.... Team briefing
.... In-house magazines

Generic competencies

9. Managing oneself

.... Personal organization
.... Time management
.... Interprersonal communication
.... Assertiveness
.... Problem solving and decision making
.... Report writing
.... Reading
.... Presentations
.... Managing stress

10. Working in the organization

.... Networking
.... Working in groups
.... Power and authority
.... Influencing
.... Negotiating

11. Getting things done

.... Setting objectives
.... Goal planning and target setting
.... Managing external consultants
.... Using statistics
.... Information technology literacy
.... Keyboard skills
.... Minute-taking
.... Record keeping
.... Setting up systems and procedures

12. Working with people

.... Interviewing
.... Listening
.... Counselling
.... Conducting and participating in meetings
.... Team building

Source: Torrington, Waite and Weightman, 1992

A pay strategy post

Appropriate professional competencies:

1 Job analysis
2 Job evaluation
2 Pay determination
2 Employee benefits
2 Peformance related pay
2 Salary administration
2 Salary structures
2 Pensions/sick pay
2 Taxation and National Insurance
3 Consultation
3 Employee involvement
3 Negotiating bodies
3 Agreement and procedures
6 Planning
6 Computer analysis

Appropriate generic competencies

9 Personal organisation
9 Interpersonal communication
9 Problem solving and decision making
9 Report writing
9 Making presentations
10 Networking
10 Influencing
11 Using statistics
11 Information technology literacy
11 Setting up systems and procedures
12 Conducting and participating in meetings

Most of the other competencies listed would probably be scored
E (no current or foreseeable need for competency in this area).
Of the competencies listed as needed, some no doubt will have
been scored A or B suggesting some difficulty. These areas need
to be prioritised for training/development.

A recruitment officer

Appropriate professional competences

1 Vacancy identification
1 Job analysis
1 Recruitment advertising
1 Selection process
1 Selection decision making
1 Letters of offer
1 Contracts of employment
1 Induction/socialisation
3 Agreements and procedures
6 Supply and demand forecasting

Appropriate generic competencies

9 Personal organisation
9 Time management
9 Interpersonal communication
12 Interviewing

The job composite model could be one way of overcoming the dilemma of whether to have general or specific competencies and whether to go for input or output analysis. It has been included here as an example of a pragmatic approach.

Individual or team competencies?

Most lists of competency concentrate on the individual. In many circumstances this is reasonable and, clearly, is essential for qualification-bearing NVQs. However, there are times when this emphasis on the individual may be counterproductive to getting work done effectively. Obvious examples are teams of foot-ballers, operating theatre teams and management teams. It is the *balance* of competencies which makes for effective performance. For example, in the second case history given in Chapter 1 (see the section, 'It takes longer than you think') it was appropriate to set team competencies for the directorate management teams.

They then needed to ensure that they covered them all and that each person had a proper job to do.

> **Questions to ask yourself**
>
> Do we want these competencies done by individuals or by a team?
>
> Does it matter which members of a team do which as long as all are covered?

National or home-grown lists of competencies?

There are national lists of competencies for almost all trades and professions under the NVQ system. Clearly this is the starting point for anyone who wishes to start drawing up a list. The advantages are that they lead to qualifications and are intended to be nationally recognised. The difficulty is that the lists are not tailormade to a particular organisation and may not reflect the particular culture and ambience that the initiative undertaken is trying to promote. They can also prove very difficult to use on occasions. Developing a home-grown list has the advantage of getting people involved in the process before the more tricky business of assessment is broached. But it would be foolish not to look at the national list and perhaps to keep some mapping of how it overlaps with any subsequent home-grown list so that if individuals want accreditation for NVQs they know where to start.

Having thought about what sort of competency you want, you are now ready to start generating the list of appropriate competencies for assessing and developing within your organisation.

References

BLOCK, P. (1987) *The Empowered Manager: Positive Political Skills at Work*, Jossey-Bass, San Francisco

BOYATZIS, R. E. (1982) *The Competent Manager: A Model for Effective Performance*, John Wiley and Sons, New York

KANTER, R. M. (1989) *When Giants Learn to Dance*, Simon & Schuster, London

INSTITUTION OF CIVIL ENGINEERS (1992) *Management Development in the Construction Industry: Guidelines for the Professional Engineer*, Thomas Telford, London

REID, M. A., BARRINGTON, H. and KENNEY, J (1992) *Training Interventions: Managing Employee Development*, 3rd edn, IPM, London

TORRINGTON, D. P., WAITE, D. and WEIGHTMAN, J. (1992) A Continuous Development Approach to Training Health Service Personnel Specialists *The Journal of European Industrial Training*, vol. 16, No 3, 3–12

WEIGHTMAN, J., BLANDAMER, W. and TORRINGTON, D. (1991) *Personnel Competences*, Report for North Western Regional Health Authority (available from the NWRHA in Manchester)

6

How Shall I Arrive at the List of Competencies?

The methodology used to arrive at the list of competencies and how they are to be assessed is determined by the purpose of using competencies. For example, if the personnel department decides to look at their own competency and try to improve the service they offer to the organisation there is unlikely to be a lot of time, money or energy available for the project. In this case, a quick look at textbooks, IPD syllabuses, other lists and asking one or two people is probably sufficient to generate an adequate list that does not leave out anything very central. Equally, assessing individuals against the list might well be by self assessment as personnel people are likely to be reasonably aware about their own performance. The important thing is to get on to the business of improvement as soon as possible, before resources run out. A quick and cheap method is what is required.

On the other hand, if the purpose of using competencies is as part of an overall cultural change tied to strategic core competencies, then far more resources are appropriately necessary. The time taken to agree the lists of competencies is an important part of getting people committed to the new culture, lists which in turn can be used in development initiatives. Here a slow, relatively thorough and thoughtful methodology would be more appropriate. So, as ever, there is no single 'right' way. The methodology needs to suit the purpose and the scale of operation.

This chapter is concerned mostly with how to arrive at the list of competencies necessary for jobs. It looks at various ways of analysing the essential competencies to do a job well. Chapter 7, in contrast, is more concerned with how we can *measure* the competencies of individuals once we have produced these lists of desirable competencies.

If after due consideration you have decided to develop home-grown lists of competencies you now have to decide now to draft the lists. Before discussing the various methods of doing this, there follows a case history of how we went about devising such a list for the management of a large health organisation (different from either of those discussed in Chapter 1). This case is included to give you a feel for the variety of issues that come up and the wide-ranging nature of such a project. The subsequent stages, of setting performance criteria and assessment methods once the competencies for the project have been agreed, are not included as it would be far too long a document.

A case history of the methods used to look at management competencies in a large health organisation

The approach we (Weightman, Butler and Griffin, 1989) took to devising a list of management competencies is that managing is rather more complex than just the observable behaviours. We argued that a variety of methods, including observation and use of competency lists, can reveal something of use to both the job holders and those that are planning management training and recruitment.

While we were doing our management competencies project there were other initiatives within the organisation associated with managing – such things as quality management initiatives, including quality circles and team briefing. For some managers these seemed to be separate initiatives, for others they were all part of a pattern of improving the work of their unit. Clearly these initiatives, approved by senior managers, indicated to job holders what sort of managing was being encouraged.

One way of exploring complex issues, such as management competencies, is to generate various questions that can be explored by different methods, which will in turn generate material that can be reintegrated to analyse the original issue. This multimedia approach has proved most popular in the study of management work (see Mintzberg, 1973; Stewart, R., 1976; Kotter, 1982 and Weightman, 1986).

We used a variety of techniques to study the work of the managers in our sample of job holders. By the use of such a range it was hoped that different aspects of the jobs would reveal themselves. It also gave us some opportunity for cross-checking various attributes. In addition, some parts of a job can only be understood in particular ways; for example, only through interview can we learn what the job holder understands, whereas only by observation can we see the degree of interruptions experienced. We used the following methods.

Agendas and networks

Before we met each person, we tried to ensure that they received a copy of Figure 6.1, Agendas and networks. This exercise is based on the work of John Kotter (1982), who looked at the work of general managers. He found that the work of managers could be understood by looking at the agendas they held and the networks they maintained to help put the agendas into effect. Effective managers had agendas made up of written and unwritten items, short and long term, and arrived at both formally and informally. Their networks often included hundreds of people, both within and outside the organisation, which were sustained through a variety of relationships. The agendas and networks form is a useful device as it looks at both the content of what managers have to do and the people with whom they get it done. We asked the people we were seeing to fill these in before we met them. Not everyone in the study received these sheets before we met them, so we collected the material in various ways: on the form as planned, verbally as part of the interview, on the forms after the interview.

Figure 6.1

Agendas and networks

Your agenda

1. List all the things you should do at work this week. Write them down as they occur to you. This should include:
   - major long-term (over one year) aims
   - short-term projects
   - regular items
   - trivia that needs to be done

2. Now add to this list all those things, big and small, that you would like to do at work this week.

3. Is there anything else that you could do at work because you want to or someone else wants you to? Add these.

---

4. How does this list fit in with the expressed plans for your department, unit or the NHS?

5. How much of this agenda is there because you want it? How much because you think it will help someone else out?

Your network

List all the individuals or groups who can affect how effective you are in your job, with whom you have a formal or informal relationship. Give both names and positions. The drawing, which may look like the one below, will describe your network.

Source: Weightman, Butler and Griffin, 1989

Semi-structured interviews

Before we started, the three of us sat down together to generate questions which we felt would elicit useful information about the work of individual jobs. Our previous experience of researching management work and critical incident interviewing were relevant here. The list we generated is given in Figure 6.2. These questions were to be used as preparation for us rather than to be gone through systematically in the interview. We were trying to hear the individual's point of view and story. By using undirected questions we were trying to get the interviewee's view of their job, not impose our view at this stage, on the basis that they were the experts on what their job was about and how they were trying to do it. Highly structured questionnaires or interviews are only appropriate when close parameters can be placed around the answers required. Our approach is more likely to motivate interviewees to cooperate than a structured questionnaire or interview as they see an opportunity to express their points of view. This approach also places more emphasis on the individual than some sort of nebulous 'average' person. Our interviews were normally two hours long.

Figure 6.2
Questions generated for the research

About agenda – with examples

Which is important and why?
Which is least important and why?
Which is most time consuming?

What prevents you from doing any of these?
What helps you to get things done?

How do you establish whether you've done something well?
What do you measure your success by?
What do you measure failure by?

How do you identify priorities?

What do you do on a regular basis – 1 per week/month?

What gives most and least satisfaction? Give examples from last year.

most .... least ....

What do you like? ....

What do you find hard? ....

Did you achieve the things listed on agenda? If not, why not?

About networks

Who
Nature of relationship
Influence
Formal/informal
Who do you go to for opinion/support/about a problem

General

What would you like to change about your job?
What is it important for you to be to get others' respect?
Where do you see yourself/like to be in 2 years?
Percentage of time spent on clinical/technical/managerial?
What is it important for you to be able to do to be a good manager?

When can I shadow you for half a day to find out the nitty gritty?
I prefer a day with least clinical work, but not too untypical.

Source: Weightman, Butler and Griffin 1989

Systematic or structured observation

Using observation gives us information about a job that is not dependent on the job holder's understanding of, ability or willingness to talk about their work. Using a systematic form for observation ensures that the observer stays alert. It can also give information for distinguishing between people, once the categories have been developed sufficiently to be reliably used by different people. We used a modification of a device developed over a period of years by Weightman (1989, see Figure 6.3 a and b).

One difficulty of observing is knowing the extent to which the process of being observed changes the behaviour of the observee. We normally asked at the end of the period, whether it had been a particularly untypical time; no one admits to having a 'typical' day. We usually spent half a day observing each person; occasionally we spent a whole day when we had the time. One person was not observed because they felt their work was too confidential.

Figure 6.3(a)
The observation schedule

We collected data in several ways on the form to try to distinguish between jobs.

Every time an activity changed we moved down a line. A change of activity is either moving to new topic or a new person. This gives a measure of how interrupted a day is. Meetings count as one activity.

We also recorded whether the person was on his or her own, face-to-face, or on the telephone, and whether the interaction was initiated by the observee or the other person.

We used the following classification:

C = clinical activities – case load
T = technical activities – using expertise for advice, policy making, research training, etc.
A = administrative activities – routine tasks, including travel; trying to get through on the phone, etc.
M = managerial activities – influencing things, nudging things along
P = personal activities – phoning home, arranging car service, etc.
S = social activities – chit chat about weather, TV, sport, etc.

Some activities had to be recorded as hybrids, e.g. T/M; we tried to keep these to a minimum. Walkabout counts as managerial. The form we used is reproduced in Figure 6.3(b).

Source: Weightman, 1989

Figure 6.3(b)
A sample observation form

Name .... Date ....

Position .... Location ....

Time	Activity	Who with/initiated by	CTAMPS work	Notes

Notes

Source: Weightman, 1989

Interview with each person's boss

We interviewed the line manager of most of the managers. This was really an exercise in crossing the Ts and dotting the Is to ensure that no important aspect of the job holder, including future needs, had been missed. We did not discuss the individual job holder. These interviews spent between 15 and 30 minutes discussing each job. We asked for the main responsibilities and task of the particular job; the relationship between that job and the line manager's job; and the way it interlinked with other jobs. If the classification of the job by our criteria was less certain, we tested it out on the line manager for his or her comments.

Other materials collected

When visiting the managers in this study we also collected, incidentally, all sorts of other material. This included copies of pamphlets produced, action item lists, lists of mail received, gossip, contact with colleagues – and endless cups of coffee. Some of these also gave us better understanding of each job.

Competency lists

The Training Agency (now called TEED) was currently (1989) working on a list of competencies. The National Health Service Training Authority, in conjunction with the Open University, had also published Lund's (1987) report about management competencies ('MESOL') geared to management training in the National Health Service (see Figure 6.4). We used this latter list in our project as it had been specifically developed within the Health Service and had associated training opportunities to go with it.

Figure 6.4
'MESOL' competencies

Managers should manage themselves, i.e. be able to:

- Manage their own managerial performance
  - set (or accept) standards of personal managerial performance
  - monitor their own performance against those standards
  - identify personal shortcomings
  - seek to achieve personal improvements

- Manage their time
  - identify the key activities in their work
  - assign suitable priorities to their activities
  - allocate their effort appropriately
  - delegate work effectively

- Manage personal stress
  - organise their work and their lives to cope with pressures
  - adjust readily to change
  - distinguish between pressure and stress
  - recognise the symptoms of personal stress
  - take appropriate actions to alleviate stress

- Adopt an appropriate management style
  - analyse accurately their environmental circumstances
  - analyse accurately the needs of the people reporting to them
  - identify their own preferred management style
  - adjust their style to the needs of their situation

- Manage their own careers
  - seek to match their personal and organisational objectives
  - keep themselves up to date
  - prepare themselves systematically for advancement
  - learn how to learn from their experiences

Managers should manage people, i.e. they should be able to:

- Select people
  - analyse jobs systematically
  - determine job requirements accurately
  - prepare accurate job descriptions
  - plan selection interviews systematically
  - conduct or participate in selection interviews effectively
  - make sound and justifiable judgements about people
  - match people to jobs and jobs to people

- Organise people
  - establish an appropriate organisational structure in their own department
  - define responsibilities clearly
  - establish accountability and reporting requirements
- Lead people
  - motivate people
  - harness their energies and efforts to get things done
  - harmonise their personal and organisational objectives
  - act appropriately to improve their performance
  - reward people in appropriate ways
- Develop people
  - identify people's needs for growth and development
  - assess their job-performances accurately and systematically
  - appraise them sensitively and constructively
  - provide them with suitable opportunities for development
  - counsel them
  - coach them
  - train them
  - support them
- Communicate with people
  - inform people (notify, report, tell, teach)
  - influence people (persuade, convince)
  - seek information from people

  accurately and succinctly in writing
    through correspondence
    reports
    papers

  confidently and effectively in speech
    through briefings
    presentations
    negotiations
    interviews
    counselling
    teaching
- Exercise discipline
  - set (or adopt) standards of behaviour and performance
  - monitor individual performances against those standards
  - take appropriate action when deviations occur
  - follow disciplinary interviews systematically
  - conduct disciplinary interviews effectively
- Handle conflict
  - deal sensitively and appropriately with grievances
  - identify accurately the causes of grievances and conflict
  - seek to harmonise where possible

- Establish working relationships
  - build strong and effective teams
  - build effective networks for information and support
  - develop alliances to facilitate work
- Conduct and participate in meetings
  - plan and organise meetings suited to their intended outcomes
  - chair meetings firmly, confidently and sensitively
  - contribute to discussions confidently and persuasively
  - record minutes in a manner appropriate for their purpose

Managers should manage their managerial jobs, i.e. they should be able to:

- Set objectives
  - interpret directives and objectives from higher authority
  - set clear and attainable objectives for their own section/department
- Forecast future requirements for their own section/department
  - scan their environment for developments that might affect them
  - identify the likely impact of future events
  - plan accordingly using appropriate planning techniques
  - assess accurately the likely resource requirements
- Obtain the required resources
  - take appropriate action to obtain the necessary resources
- Exercise control (over resources, performance, output and quality)
  - establish control systems
  - operate budgets
  - control stocks
  - establish standards which are attainable and acceptable
  - monitor performance against those standards
  - take appropriate action to correct deviations and discrepancies
  - adopt suitable ways of improving performance, output and quality
- Deal with problems (and opportunities) as they arise
  - analyse problems and opportunities systematically
  - identify their needs for further information
  - assemble information from available resources
  - cope with uncertainty
  - generate practicable solutions
  - evaluate potential solutions systematically against agreed criteria
  - reach justifiable decisions
  - manage the implementation of those decisions

- Manage change
  - cope with imposed change
  - initiate necessary changes in their own organisation
  - plan for the smooth implementation of change
  - identify and take account of the predictable impacts of change
  - apply change-management techniques to accomplish change

Managers should manage in their environment, i.e. they should be able to:

- Cope with problems stemming from the organisation in which they work
  - unsuitable organisational structures
  - unclear or overlapping responsibilities
  - inadequate communication flows
  - boundary frictions between different departments
  - incongruent objectives
  - conflicting imperatives
  - conflicting perspectives
  - different timescales
  - different cultures, values, languages in other departments
- Take due account, in the way they manage, of factors within their organisation
  - organisational objectives
  - organisational constraints
  - organisational policies
  - organisational norms
  - organisational culture
  - organisational politics
- Take due account, in the way they manage, of factors outside their organisation
  - the primacy of the interests of the patient/client
  - the impact of the local context in which they are working
  - the impact of the national context
  - the law as it affects health care provision and management
  - the economy and the provision of resources
  - health economics
  - the potential impact of demographic trends locally and nationally
  - sociological trends and rising expectations
  - the impact of technological developments on health care provision and management
- Influence the organisational 'tone' of their own section/department
  - adopt a suitable management style
  - establish appropriate standards in an appropriate way
  - monitor standards closely

Source: Lund, 1987

Who was included in the study?

There is no general definition of how individuals are classified as managers. Who is included in the category of management often has as much to do with salary and status as the work that any individual does. When studying management competencies, or any other aspect of management, it is often advisable to leave it to the organisation involved to suggest who they consider to be managers.

I have provided this detailed history really to show that there are various decisions to be made along the way and that the practice of arriving at a list of competencies is not an exact science – it includes a lot of judgement and interpretation. You will undoubtedly disagree with some of what we did. For example, if I was doing the same project now there would be other lists of competencies to use and, working with other people, we might well come up with different questions. I might also seek the views of peers and subordinates about the tasks of the job as well as the boss. So what *are* the principal methods for arriving at competencies?

Existing lists – modified

There are so many existing lists of competencies these days it is hard to imagine that there is any job left which does not have some sort of competencies list, somewhere. It would be absurd not to least to look at these.

Questions to ask yourself

Where can I get hold of some appropriate lists?
– the national bodies
– other similar organisations to us
– professional bodies
– employers' organisations
– trade unions?

How were the lists arrived at?
– were they made up without reference to research?
– were they based on detailed study?

93

What attempts have been made to get acceptance of these lists?
What credibility do they have within the organisation/ profession/group?

How closely do the people the list was made for resemble my group?

Do I want to adopt one of these lists wholesale and save the time and effort to use elsewhere?
Do I want to just adapt one of these lists?

How important is the process of creating the list to the implementation of the list?

The advantage of taking an existing list wholesale is the obvious saving in time and effort. However, it means missing out on the process of gaining commitment from those who create something together which may prove costly at the implementation stage. An imposed solution can be a focus for creative reasons for *not* doing it. A brought-in list can sometimes be not quite right.

Personal construct theory and repertory grid techniques

Personal construct theory was developed by Kelly (1955). He argues that people understand their own experiences through the constructions they use to analyse them, and use these constructs to anticipate events. The constructions vary from individual to individual and thus Kelly assumes that all facts are subject to alternative constructions. Kelly developed two techniques to measure individuals' constructs – the 'repertory grid' technique, which measures the mathematical relationship between constructs, and 'self-characterisation', which gives a qualitative account of a person's view of his or herself.

For the purposes of studying competencies the first part of the repertory grid technique is useful to study how people view their job – what constructs are they using to analyse their jobs and the relative importance of the various aspects of their jobs. This approach emphasises the individual rather than the average. The cumulative evidence from individuals is felt by many to be more powerful than the lowest common factor of seeking averages.

Figure 6.5

Repertory grid questions (after A. and V. Stewart, 1976)

You need sheets of paper or cards and then ask the following questions.

1. Name an activity you perform in your job that is very important – not a role or responsibility, but a verb.

2. Name an activity you do frequently – not necessarily important but occupies a good deal of time.

3. Name an activity that, though important, is unlikely to appear in your diary.

4. Give me two more examples of stage 1.

5. Give me two more examples of stage 2.

6. Obviously I want the highlights of your job – is any activity missing?

7. The next stage is to give various combinations of these eight responses in groups of three and ask, 'In what way do two of these activities resemble each other that makes them different from the third'. Do this several times, say five or six, with different combinations.

8. Look at the constructs, the products of stage 7, in pairs and ask, 'Which is more important in your job to do well, A or B?' Do this several times until you are no longer getting new constructs.

9. Do the same thing as in stage 8, asking which you get more satisfaction out of doing.

The output of this activity gives you an insight into what the job holder sees as the important and satisfying dimensions of the job. This can give you some of the core individual competencies if you are taking an input approach. Clearly this is quite a time-consuming approach but is given here in detail for those occasions when you have the resources to do a thorough job. It can also be used more informally to suggest questions in interviews.

Interviews

There are three sorts of interviews:

- Structured, when there is a list of questions to which answers are sought, rather like a questionnaire answered face-to-face.
- Semi-structured, where the interviewer has a list of topics and questions to cover but is prepared to follow insights and issues raised by the interviewee.
- Unstructured, where the questioning is non-directive rather like a psychotherapeutic interview where the agenda is entirely that of the interviewee.

For competencies investigation, interviews are most likely to be structured or semi-structured.

Interviews are useful ways of exploring competencies as they allow a discussion of the topics considered by the interviewer and, if a semi-structured interview is used, also allow the exploration of any other issues that the interviewee may consider important. This can be particularly useful during the initial phase of deciding what the competencies are. As Bannister and Fransella say:

'It is interesting that psychologists seem always to have been suspicious of the value of direct personal statements. They make their tests oblique so that what is measured is obscured from the subject. They embed the scales in their questionnaires on the assumption that man is a deceiving creature. Yet many of us might feel that we have something meaningful to say (perhaps even scientifically meaningful) concerning ourselves and what we have been about.'

Bannister and Fransella (1971), p. 79

The sorts of questions you might use in a competency interview may include some of those given in the case history above. A mixture of closed and open questions seems to be the most fruitful. You need the details of what they do, but you also need some of their interpretations of what they do. It is useful to generate a few questions before interviewing which you can to refer to when there is a pause in the conversation.

Interviews have several advantages over questionnaires: you can rephrase questions if they are not understood; people are more motivated to respond to an interview than a questionnaire; it is possible to get quite a lot of information in an hour from each person. However, each additional person probably adds less and less extra information and understanding to the process. The obvious disadvantages are that some sort of censorship can be at work – interviewees will not mention the embarrassing, secret or obscure parts of their jobs. Confidentiality is, thus, necessary. It is also difficult for individuals being interviewed to translate reality into abstraction or to remember all that they did.

The other issue concerns who to interview about job competencies.

Questions to ask yourself

How far should I trawl?
– the jobholder(s)?
– the boss?
– the colleagues?
– the subordinates?
– important figures in the network?
– professional bodies?
– trade unions?

The answer will, again, depend on the scale of the project, the resources available, and the consequences of getting the competencies list wrong. A variation is to get a group of job holders together and interview them collectively to get a discussion going about the topic of competencies. This has the advantage of saving time but loses the individual contributions and requires good group management skills to keep the discussion focused.

Observation

Sometimes there are behaviours essential to doing the job which do not get talked about in interviews and do not appear elsewhere. It is only when we start observing that they come to the fore, for example, the ability of operation managers to deal with constant interruption. Some period of observation is useful, if resources and access permit, as it can give you the feel of a job as well as more precise information.

Most people use fairly informal procedures of observation and questioning to obtain information on social behaviour and personalities. These processes are taken for granted and there is little conscious awareness of doing them. If we want to use observation to arrive at competencies, or indeed assess people against these competencies, we need to become aware of the processes so we can use the knowledge systematically. The impressions we form are influenced by various factors: the patterns of inference we are accustomed to making; personal tendencies to either moderate or extreme judgements about the attributes of others; sensitivity we possess towards particular observational cues or classes of cues such as voice, physical features or movement. You can probably think of lots of other personal factors that could lead to inaccurate assessments. There is the additional problem that our memory is not accurate for very long.

For all these reasons, structuring the observation in some way is useful. The chief advantage of structured or systematic observation over other methods is, as Scott points out:

> 'that, unlike interviewing it allows the researcher to record behaviour as it occurs and thus free him from dependence on the respondent's ability or willingness to describe his actions.'
>
> Scott (1965), p. 286

The important parameter of systematic observation is whether the set criteria can differentiate among types of behaviour.

There are various ways of drawing up an observation schedule; one that works is the following.

1. Decide the categories of behaviour to be observed. For example, if we want to study the competencies of receptionists in a hotel, we could guess that we need at least some categories on dealing with people face-to-face, answering the telephone, coping with the computer, dealing with queries, briefing the next shift, and so on. These could then be broken down further. Referring to existing lists and/or the results of interviews are good starting points. Another example is given in Figure 6.6, of the core competencies sought by one local education authority for heads of departments in schools.

Figure 6.6

Core competencies for LEA Heads of Department

1. VISION
    (a) Ability to seek goals & desire appropriate objectives
    (b) Able to perform beyond the immediate needs of the situation
    (c) Able to predict the need for appropriate tasks
    (d) Producing original, expressive or imaginative responses to tasks
    (e) Able to demonstrate an awareness of value dimensions and preparedness to challenge assumptions

2. PLANNING SKILLS
    (a) Able to forward plan to meet a target
    (b) Able to judge a range of alternative strategies before implementing a plan
    (c) Able to be aware of appropriate timescale
    (d) Ability to prioritise
    (e) Ability to analyse into discrete elements
    (f) Ability to sequence appropriate strategies
    (g) Ability to take account of the need for contingency plans
    (h) Ability to develop detailed and logically sequenced plans to accomplish goals

3. CRITICAL THINKING
    (a) Ability to think analytically and systematically
    (b) Ability to apply concepts and principles to a problem
    (c) Ability to differentiate between intuitive and analytical thinking
    (d) Lateral thinking

4. LEADERSHIP SKILL
    (a) Ability to direct the actions of others towards an agreed goal
    (b) Structuring interaction to the purposes in hand
    (c) Arranging the effective deployment of resources
    (d) Willingness to accept responsibility
        (i) for the actions of others
        (ii) for achievements of goals
    (f) Ability to act decisively in appropriate situations

5. PERSISTENCE
    (a) Preparedness to make use of a range of strategies to achieve a problem solution
    (b) Ability to demonstrate a commitment to task completion
    (c) Ability to recognise when circumstances require a flexible response

6. INFLUENCE SKILLS
   (a) Ability to have an impact on others by action or example
   (b) Ability to get others involved in the processes of management
   (c) Persuading staff to balance individual needs and institutional requirements
   (d) Persuading others to consider a wide range of options
   (e) Able to negotiate effectively
   (f) Ability to use a range of strategies to obtain agreement

7. INTERPERSONAL RELATIONSHIPS
   (a) Ability to establish and maintain positive relationships
   (b) Ability to perceive the needs, concerns and personal circumstances of others
   (c) Able to recognise and resolve conflict
   (d) Able to use effective listening skills
   (e) Able to notice, interpret and respond to non-verbal behaviour
   (f) Able to make effective use of a range of oral and written communication skills
   (g) Ability to give appropriate feedback in a sensitive manner

8. SELF-CONFIDENCE
   (a) Able to feel assured about personal ability and judgement
   (b) Ability to demonstrate assertive behaviour without generating hostility
   (c) Ability to seek and accept feedback about personal performance and management style
   (d) Able to offer a challenge to others in order to enhance their self-confidence

9. DEVELOPMENT
   (a) Able to actively find ways of enhancing self-knowledge
   (b) Able to demonstrate an understanding of learning style (in self and others)
   (c) Able to actively seek opportunities to enhance growth in self and others
   (d) Ability to assess development needs
   (e) Ability to design, implement and evaluate development programmes
   (f) Able to implement a positive climate conducive to growth and development

10. EMPATHY
    (a) Ability to demonstrate awareness of the needs of the group
    (b) of the needs of an individual
    (c) Ability to listen and communicate in a constructive manner
    (d) Able to indicate sensitivity to the implications of decisions (for others)

11. STRESS TOLERANCE
    (a) Able to demonstrate appropriate behaviour in stressful circumstances
    (b) Able to demonstrate resilience in pressure situations
    (c) Able to remain effective in a range of working situations
    (d) Able to maintain a balance between priorities
    (e) Able to take into account level of stress in others

2. Pilot these categories with one or two short observations to see if they are workable. Usually some rejigging is required. New categories, amalgamations, and unravellings and rejections are all quite common at this stage.
3. Design an observation sheet which requires an entry either at set time intervals or when the person being observed changes activity. Alternatively, design one which is suitable to be used when going round a group of people recording what they are doing when observed. An observation sheet is essential to maintain vigilance in the observer; it is very easy to get distracted by what is going on. For example, in using Figure 6.6 the observer was expected to watch three people in an assessment centre and move round them systematically.
·4. Have room on the sheet to make odd notes of things seen or heard while doing the observation as these may inform the analysis later.
5. Do the observation by appearing as low key as possible both in dress and manner, with minimum eye contact and gestures. Try not to get involved in discussions with the observee. Concentrate on the recording form and start as soon as possible after arriving.
6. Ask the observee at the end of the session whether it has been a particularly unusual session. No one in my experience ever admits to having a typical day so I ask if it is particularly

untypical! But there is a genuine difficulty over what is a representative sample of time – to which there is no entirely satisfactory response.

7. If the observation is being used to decide on a competency list, the information gained will then need to be put with material from other sources to arrive at the list. Similarly, if the observation is being used in assessment it will need to be put with other observations and material collected elsewhere. No judgement can be made safely on the basis of one observation.

There are several problems involved in doing observations. One is the length of time it takes to get access to people – they can be very nervous of being observed. The observations are also very time consuming to do as they normally need at least half a day per person. So it is really only feasible for small numbers. There is the added difficulty of knowing to what extent the very process of being observed changes the behaviour of the observee. Observation is obviously incapable of assessing non-observable activities such as planning or thinking. Also, it is not a technique that can be rushed. However, observation has enormous benefits in giving lots of the little details people forget to mention and a general 'feel' for the job.

Questionnaires

Questionnaires have to have predetermined categories which prescribe what the respondent can communicate about. They are more likely to be used in the latter stages of arriving at a list of competencies when you have a fairly good idea of what to include. They have the great advantage of being a cheap way of sampling a large number of people. If, for example, you are trying to test a list of competencies against a large body of people it might be appropriate to send out a questionnaire with the list that has a tick box against each item, along the following lines:

This is something I need to do frequently in my job	☐
This is something I need to do occasionally in my job	☐
This is something I need to do rarely in my job	☐
I could anticipate having to do this in the future	☐
I never need to do this in my job	☐

The results could then be collated to see which items on the list of competencies practitioners feel are necessary to their jobs now and possibly in the future.

Functional analysis

If you have decided to take an outputs approach to competencies then your main method of arriving at the list will be through functional analysis. Essentially, this involves repeating the question, 'What do you need to do to be able to do that?' This process is continued until you arrive at small enough behaviours to be useful. If the competency required is an ability to fillet white fish, the sequence might go something like:

Able to get fish in correct position.
Able to use knife in the appropriate direction
Set a suitable standard of lack of bones and tidy-looking fillet.
Do all this in a reasonable amount of time.

To each of these, in turn the question, 'What do you need to do to be able to do that' could be posed until a suitable level of detail is acquired.

The main issue is how to arrive at the answer to this question. It may be appropriate to involve a range of people in your discussion. You may decide to use some of the above methods to answer your main question. Very often skilled people will be able to break the behaviours into smaller ones by trying it themself and recording what they do. Self observation using a video may be helpful here. Once you have what looks like a sensible list based on functional analysis it makes some sense to test this out with experienced job holders. Ask for their views using a questionnaire, group discussion or interview.

Consultancy skills

For most circumstances, and particularly where an inputs approach is adopted, a mixture of methods would seem most useful as different methods answer the disadvantages of each other. As McCall et al. concluded about management behaviour:

> For describing managerial behaviour, no method clearly shows itself superior for all potential research circumstances and settings. The use of multiple methods should allow the researcher to capitalize on the combined strengths of a collectivity. If a description can be shown to agree with those provided by complementary methods, then it contains a degree of accuracy, unattainable by a description that is consistent with only one method.
>
> McCall et al. (1978), p. 33

Similarly, when studying competencies, it would seem that a more robust list will emerge if a variety of methods are used to research the area. Which methods to use will depend on the scale of the operation as much as anything. Where it is crucial, and the resources have been agreed, then time-consuming methods such as observation and interviewing can be done thoroughly. Where it is a smaller, more local project there is likely to be more dependence on existing lists with local modification in the light of a few interviews or questionnaires.

All the above methods depend for their success on the ability of the researcher to establish working relationships with those researched. The emphasis is on the respondents; only when they feel that they can trust and rely on the confidentiality of the interview or observation will insightful gems be revealed. Because of this need for trust and confidentiality many organisations have found it useful to use outside consultants. But internal consultants can be just as effective, and may often have higher credibility than those from outside and are likely to pick up on small things more quickly. A useful book on the processes of consultancy is Casey (1993).

References

BANNISTER, D. and FRANSELLA, F. (1971) *Inquiring Man: The Theory of Personal Constructs*, Penguin, Harmondsworth

CASEY, D. (1993) *Managing Learning in Organizations*, Open University Press, Milton Keynes

KELLY, G. A. (1955) *The Psychology of Personal Constructs*, Morton, New York

KOTTER, J. (1982) *The General Managers*, The Free Press, New York

LUND, B. (1987) *Better Management*, Report 1, 2 and 3, The Open University and NHSTA

McCALL, M. W., MORRISON, A. M. and HANNAN, R. L. (1978) *Studies of Managerial Work: Results and Methods*, Centre for Creative Leadership, North Carolina

MINTZBERG, H. (1973) *The Nature of Managerial Work*, Harper and Row, London

SCOTT, W. R. (1965) Field Methods in the Study of Organisations, in *Handbook of Organisations* (ed. J. G. March), Rand McNally, Chicago, 262–300

STEWART, A. and STEWART, V. (1976) *Tomorrow's Men Today*, IPM, London

STEWART, R. (1976) *Contrasts in Management*, McGraw-Hill, Maidenhead

WEIGHTMAN, J. (1986) *Middle Management: Dinosaur or Dynamo*, Ph.D thesis, UMIST

WEIGHTMAN, J. (1989) The Balance of Work for Senior Staff in Secondary Schools, *Schools Organisation*, **9** (1) 121–9

WEIGHTMAN, J., BUTLER, L. and GRIFFIN, J. (1989) *Management Competences in Tameside and Glossop District Health Authority*, Unpublished

7

Can I Measure Competency?

Once you have decided on an appropriate list of competencies the next stage is to decide how you will measure people's competency against this list. Measuring anything about people inevitably means judging them in some way. The competency approach is a way of trying to reduce the subjective nature of this judgement but there will always be some point when someone has to judge another against the competencies listed. Where this judgement is to last a long time, and may affect the individual's chances in employment or education, very careful consideration of the assessment process is necessary. This may explain why you can find almost mystical discussions of the assessment process in education journals. It also accounts for the extraordinarily elaborate assessment procedures associated with NVQs. Such educational and qualification types of assessment are outside the scope of this book and I would refer those who are interested in these details to TEED, Lloyd and Cook (1993) or Fletcher (1991). This chapter is aimed at those who want to get on with a practical approach to assessing competencies within the organisation, where the judgements are important but can be modified as time goes on.

Using a competency approach does not change some of the basic questions that have to be asked about any sort of assessment. This chapter seeks to clarify these basic questions which concern essentially, how we judge the performance of another and how we record it. Using competencies tries to clarify what performance we are trying to judge but we still have to make the judgement. This chapter looks at the issues surrounding different ways of doing this.

Questions to ask yourself

Why are we assessing this person?
- to recruit them?
- to develop them?
- to promote them?
- to redeploy them?
- to gain national qualifications?

How important is it that the assessment is very accurate?

Is the assessment compulsory?

How much time and effort are we prepared to put into the process?

How frequently do we want the assessment done?

Who should do the judging?
- the person themselves?
- their colleagues?
- someone within a position of authority?
- someone with expertise?
- a variety of people?

What sort of evidence is needed to assess the competency?
- can the individual collect written materials to prove they have done something?
- must the competency be observed?
- are simulated exercises appropriate for assessing these competencies?
- can the competency be demonstrated during normal work?

Who has sight of the conclusions of the assessment?
- is it confidential?
- just the individual, their line manager and personnel records?
- can the information be used for purposes other than the original?
- should the assessment result be used outside the unit?

What will happen as a result of the assessment?
Who is responsible for ensuring this follow up takes place?

Some of these questions are dealt with in other chapters; for example, *why assess* is the focus of Chapters 3 and 4; *what happens as a result* of the assessment is the focus of Chapter 8.

Other questions can really only be discussed within the particular setting. For example, issues concerning who has sight of the assessment and the use it is put tò are far more likely to be raised in public-sector organisations, such as education and health, where there is a tradition of pluralism and a lot of professions. Alternatively, unitarist, commercial companies which operate with a non-union policy are more likely to have human resources approaches to these issues, where the information goes on the personal file to be used when appropriate. But it is worth asking the questions even if the answer is, 'No problem here'. To which others may retort, 'Says who?'

This chapter concentrates on who should do the assessing and what should be assessed; the two sets of questions are related. The nature of the evidence collected will depend on who is doing the assessment and the resources available to them. For example, self assessment permits access to all of the working life of the person, but the issue is how to demonstrate that the assessment is valid. If the assessment is to include peer assessment, it becomes time consuming and detracts from regular work so a consequent issue is how to resource this appropriately. If there is to be an assessment centre, questions have to be answered about who the appropriate people to run it are and what the nature of the exercises should be. Where national lists of competencies are involved, with an associated national qualification, serious attention has to be given to the assessment procedures as these are laid down in detail and can take a lot of effort to understand.

First, let us consider who should do the assessment.

Self assessment

Many lists of competency start being compiled with some sort of self assessment. Job holders are given a list of a wide range of competencies and their behavioural descriptions and asked to rate each one in terms of its importance for effective performance of their job. This approach is predicated on the premise that job holders know something about how to get the job done that others do not. It seems logical then to include some sort of self assessment when we are assessing individual job holders' competency, as they presumably know something about the way they perform that others do not.

Self assessment can be done by a simple series of questions after each behavioural description such as:

I have difficulty doing this
I sometimes have difficulty doing this
I can usually to this
I do not need to do this at present

It can also be done by asking people to keep a diary, with examples of times when they were demonstrating particular competencies. So, over a week, they may seek to record examples of competency in such things as influencing or communication and jot down when they observe themselves doing so.

Another form of self assessment is to collect evidence of having done activities which demonstrate the competency. This is particularly used for the NVQ system. It can comprise a record book or log book, where particular experiences are listed, and copies of tasks, minutes of meetings attended and diagrams are included. For example, engineering apprentices who will become technicians in a university keep such log books. They have diagrams of how to maintain the different systems they have worked on, such as the gas supplies to chemistry or the wiring system in the computer department. These act as a record of what they have done and, incidentally, also act as an aide-mémoire if they have to do the same thing again. The NVQ assessors can then look at these log books and ask the individual questions about them.

The current system of records of achievement which school children keep are a foundation for this approach. There has also been a long tradition in the engineering profession of keeping a log book of experiences and attainments. It is likely that more people will expect to keep this sort of record in the future. This is especially likely if moving between employers becomes the norm rather than staying long term with one employer (who in the past kept the records). These log books can provide evidence of competency which could be mapped (see 'Mapping' below) against a list of competency.

The advantages of self assessment are:

1. It emphasises self development and an individual's responsibility to ensure their own competency. This fits in with the model of being a professional.
2. It uses the individual's detailed understanding of the job and how they perform it.
3. It is economical in time and effort.

The disadvantages of self assessment are:

1. It is liable to excessive subjectivity.
2. It is uneven – some will be overly harsh on themselves and others over generous.
3. It needs some sort of external validation if the competency assessment is to be used for important judgements.

Peer assessment

Formal assessment by our colleagues is not very common in the workplace; informal assessment of competency by colleagues is very common. It would seem logical to include some form of peer assessment of competency where the competencies include aspects of team working. Only those who work alongside us really know whether we have made substantial contributions, whether of content or process, to the outcomes of a group activity. Why not assess this by asking the colleagues?

A starting point is often to ask how competent we, as a group, are and what needs to be improved. For example, after meetings questions may be asked about the process side of the meeting to see if anything can be done to make meetings more effective. From this collective assessment of group competency, it is still quite a big move to assessing individual competency by peers. But there are several ways of making this move.

It can be done by straightforwardly asking the team members to rank order everyone in the group for their contribution against the various competencies; this overcomes individual prejudices. It can be done by using a similar list of questions as for self assessment, against each competency and each member. Alternatively, you may ask individuals to record specific incidents where a colleague has demonstrated a particular competency.

A group of headteachers were trying to develop a suitable form of appraisal for heads. They arrived at the idea of having an agreed list of competencies which each of them used to visit each other's school. They worked in self-selected pairs and spent two days in each other's school, looking at what was going on and talking to whoever they wished, particularly the deputy headteachers. At the end of this period they had a discussion with each other about the findings and then set targets for the next two years.

The advantages of peer assessment are:

1. It includes a contribution from the group or team.
2. It encourages a collective responsibility for developing competency.
3. Individuals can feel they are talking to someone who really understands their job, where these are similar.

The disadvantages of peer assessment are:

1. It is time consuming.
2. It is dependent on the credibility and trust of those involved.
3. It may be counter-cultural to be assessed by colleagues and may require a great deal of preparation where the assessment is to be of an individual.

Boss assessment

This is certainly the most common form of performance assessment practised in organisations, both formally and informally. The rise of performance appraisal schemes over the past 20 years has made the idea of being formally assessed by our boss familar to most of us. Using a competency approach to this is really an attempt to be more objective and systematic. In most cases, it is giving the boss a model on which to base the assessment.

The assessment process itself may include a formal period of observation, exercises and collecting evidence. In most organisations it does not and the assessment is more informal, with the boss using the list of competencies and memory of the individual's performance over time to check the list. Sometimes this is modified by having a 'grandparent' – a boss at a more senior level – who checks the assessment to ensure there are no gross discrepancies between sections and individual managers.

As an example, in one pharmaceutical company they have job profile sheets for each job (see Figure 7.1). The managers use the sheets to assess individuals through feedback and noted behaviours throughout the year. Where there is a performance gap, they may make its development a specific objective in the annual performance management interview but usually it would be dealt with in a development plan and achieved through coaching (see Chapter 8 for further discussion of these).

Figure 7.1
Job profile sheet

Job title

Purpose ....

Responsibility ....

Skills	**Knowledge**
Technical and specific listed here for each job profile.	Technical and specific listed here for each job profile.

Competencies
Various behavioural statements of transferable skills such as communication and influencing

---

The advantages of boss assessment are:

1. The boss is responsible for the competency of the section so is likely to be committed to developing the competency of employees.
2. As line managers they are seen as having a legitimate right to assess – both by the organisation and the individual – and the process enhances this.
3. The boss should have some idea of what those working for him or her can do.

The disadvantages of boss assessment are:

1. Bosses do not always know the detailed competencies involved in each of the jobs of those working for them.
2. It can be very time consuming if there are a lot of people in the section and a detailed competency list.
3. The level of credibility and trust is not always sufficient.
4. Ensuring comparability between bosses can be difficult as some have all swans and others all geese.

Any others?

Specialist staff in personnel and training departments will be useful in looking at the competencies of individuals. Most organisations have moved away from them doing so directly; they are more often seen as a resource to consult about the process and for training others to do the assessment. Equally, even more specialist staff exist in very large organisations or in consultancy companies who specialise in competency assessment. Some TECs can provide some of this sort of advice for smaller companies.

It is always worth asking whether anyone else should be involved in the assessment process, for example, outside agencies where someone works in several settings. Getting expert opinion from outside may be helpful if the particular competency is rare in the organisation. Examples of people to ask include professional bodies, further and higher educational establishments, consultancy companies specalising in the area, trade unions on issues such as Health and Safety at Work and NVQ assessors.

We have discussed the usual people to be involved in assessing competencies in organisations. Sometimes it may be appropriate to use several sources of information where the assessment needs to be particularly accurate. Usually this is far too extravagant a use of resources and a perfectly adequate assessment is made by one person and can be modified as things go along. Let us now look at different ways of actually doing the assessment.

Observation

As we discussed in Chapter 6, there are several sorts of observation. There are two ways it can be used for assessing competencies. First is the informal observation which we all use to get information about the behaviour of others to arrive at our judgements about them. Second is systematic observation, where we go out of our way to see them doing the behaviour being assessed. We then make our judgement about whether they have actually achieved the performance criteria of the competency. We may make a special appointment to do this or drop in on a normal working period when we know the behaviour is likely to be occurring.

The advantages of observation are:

1. You actually see the behaviour to be judged.
2. It has a high face validity and so a high credibility.

The disadvantages of observation are:

1. It is very time consuming.
2. It can be inhibiting for the observed.
3. There is a real difficulty in knowing when to sample the particular event. Individuals will often say, 'If only you had come last week it was quite different.'

Assessment or development centres

Assessment or development centres are when individuals come together for a period of a day or two to take part in a series of exercises where the performance of individuals is assessed by observers. Historically these have been used for selection, for example the selection of army officers during the Second World War or senior grades of the Civil Service since then – indeed, they still are used for this purpose in many organisations. They are also used for assessing people for promotion and as a basis for indicating what needs developing in individuals. They were originally designed, according to Dulewicz (1989), to predict an individual's potential rather than to assess current performance.

They have been particularly popular for assessing people for, or in, senior management positions.

Once the competencies to be assessed have been agreed, a series of exercises where these competencies can be demonstrated has to be devised. Typically these will include a series of role play exercises, individual exercises and discussions where general, transferable competencies are concerned. The training of the assessors is then crucial; they need to be able to assess the competencies in question reliably. A useful book on assessment centres is Woodruffe (1994).

An example of a development centre is that run by several local education authorities based on the core competencies reproduced in Figure 6.6. This was run on each occasion for two days with the following agenda. The delegates were divided into groups of six for the joint exercises and each observer observed two or three of them throughout the period. The observers were practising headteachers.

Development centre agenda

Day one

16.30–17.00	Arrival and registration
17.00	Introduction
17.30	Activity 1: Discussion of educational topics in groups of six. This was seen as an ice breaker and a means of looking at individuals' knowledge.
18.30	Dinner
19.45	Activity 2: Written individual activity about appointing a deputy head. This was to see if they thought through what was necessary and could communicate this succinctly.
20.30	Activity 3: A group activity or game on a non-educational topic. This was to see how they performed in groups and in decision making.
21.30	Activity 4: Negotiation of topics for the next day from a given list for Activity 5. To look at negotiating skills.

Day two

08.00	Breakfast
08.45	Activity 5: Presentation of topics. Ten minutes to do so. To look at organisation of time and presentation skills.
10.00	Activity 6: Interviews in groups of three with one giving feedback. Role play of real interview situations such as appraisal, counselling and discipline. To look at interpersonal skills.
11.00	Coffee
11.15	Activity 7: Chairing a meeting, with 15 minutes to come to a decision. Six problems for groups of six. Everyone has a go then 15 minutes for peer group feedback.
12.30	Lunch
13.30	Activity 7 continued (three before and three after lunch).
14.30	Activity 8: In-tray exercise as an individual with a range of topics that might come to a school headteacher to deal with. To examine the appropriateness of the prioritising and their response.
15.30	Tea
15.45	Individual interviews with observers, using inventories as described in Figure 6.6. Discussion of what can be done about the results.

The advantages of assessment/development centres are:

1. They focus attention on the individual for the period of the centre.
2. They allow exposure to a variety of activities which may not occur in the workplace and so meaningful assessment of potential is more likely.
3. They usually involve people other than the individual's own line manager in the assessment.

The disadvantages of assessment/development centres are:

1. They are expensive to run.
2. They are a simulation rather than the real thing.
3. They can only include exercises that are physically possible to put on away from the workplace so some important competencies may not be covered.
4. They need to be followed up to ensure that something results from the assessment.

Portfolios – documentation and recording

A major source of evidence of competency for the NVQ procedures of assessment is portfolios of documentation to demonstrate the individual's achievements. These can be a development of the 'Records of Achievement' started in school where the individual records things they have done and has this countersigned by someone responsible for the event. It can be a log book as described above in the section on self assessment. Alternatively, it can be a portfolio of different documents such as copies of meetings attended, course syllabuses undertaken, documents worked on with examples of work the individual has completed, letters of recommendation from colleagues, and other appropriate materials the individual sees fit to produce.

The advantages of portfolios are:

1. The individual is responsible for this portfolio and decides what to include.
2. It is a record of achievement or competency, not a record of attempts or failure.
3. It emphasises continuous development and life-long learning.

The disadvantages of portfolios are:

1. They are difficult to contain and it can be hard to decide how much documentation to produce.
2. Inevitably this approach to assessment can be very time consuming to sift through and assess.
3. There can be issues of confidentiality involved that mean some important experiences at work cannot be demonstrated publicly.

Mapping

Mapping is the term used to describe the process of comparing the list of competencies with the opportunities, experiences and abilities of those being assessed. It is perhaps easiest to give an example to demonstrate this.

We (Torrington, Weightman and Peacock, 1992) mapped the opportunities available to students studying science and engineering at The University of Manchester Institute of Science and Technology (UMIST) to collect evidence towards the national MCI competency-based standards for management. We looked in detail at the syllabuses and asked members of staff questions about the courses (see Figure 7.2). Our overall findings were that undergraduate courses had several possibilities for students to start collecting evidence towards MCI standard I. The courses reviewed were in the Departments of Chemical Engineering (CHEM), Electrical Engineering (ELEC), Mechanical Engineering (MECH), Civil Engineering (CIVIL), Textiles (TEXTL), Material Science (MATERL) and Chemistry (CHEMRY).

The charts reproduced in Figure 7.2 were based on such details from the syllabuses as:

- Communications (25 hours) – writing skills, wordprocessor and spreadsheet skills, elementary statistics, literature searching.
- Process Economics and Simulation (50 hours) – including: flowsheets, sizing and costing, economic models and evaluation of projects, investment appraisal techniques: payback, time/value/money, inflation.
- Organisational Behaviour (25 hours) – selection, training, motivation, communication, leading, organisational change.
- Engineering Design and Safety (50 hours) – including: safety legislation.
- Marketing (Management Standard II) (50 hours).
- Legal and Administrative Systems for Pollution Control (25 hours).
- Work placements – over half the students take placements in industry.
- Third Year Group Design Project (125 hours) – projects come from industry and include tender: cost estimations, markets,

Figure 7.2
Mapping UMIST courses to the MCI standards

	CHEM	ELEC	MECH	CIVIL	TEXTL	MATERL	CHEMRY
Manage operations							
Maintain operations							
1.1 for Quality							
1.2 for Productive work							
Contribute to change							
2.1 Evaluation	X	X	X	X	X		
2.2 Implementation							
Manage finance							
Expenditure and resources							
3.1 Recommendations	X	X	X	X	X		
3.2 Monitor and control							
Managing people							
Recruitment							
4.1 Define requirements							
4.2 Selection							
Develop people							
5.1 Teams	X	X	X	X	X	X	
5.2 Individuals							
5.3 Oneself							
Plan work							
6.1 Set objectives	X	X	X	X	X	X	X
6.2 Plan work methods		X					
6.3 Allocate work		X					
6.4 Provide feedback		X					
Enhance relationships							
7.1 with Subordinates							
7.2 with Manager	X	X	X	X	X	X	X
7.3 with Colleagues	X	X	X	X	X	X	X
7.4 Minimise conflict		X					
7.5 Discipline/grievance							
7.6 Counsel staff							
Manage information							
Evaluate information							
8.1 to aid Decisions	X	X	X	X	X	X	X
8.2 Record and store it	X	X	X	X	X	X	X
Exchange information							
9.1 Lead meetings		X					
9.2 Contribute	X	X	X	X	X	X	
9.3 Advise and inform							

KNOWLEDGE AND UNDERSTANDING

Principles and methods	CHEM	ELEC	MECH	CIVIL	TEXTL	MATERL	CHEMRY
C Legislation	X	X	X	X	X	–	X
D Defining competencies	–	–	–	–	–	–	–
E Recruitment	X	X	–	–	X	–	–
F Motivation and delegation	X	X	X	X	X	X	–
G Working with others	X	X	X	X	X	X	–
H Staff development	–	–	–	–	–	–	–
I Teams	X	X	X	X	X	–	–
J Operations	X	X	X	X	X	X	X
K Change and innovation	X	X	–	–	X	–	–
L Marketing (Std II)	X	X	X	–	X	X	–
M Finance	X	X	X	X	X	X	X
N Accessing and storing information	X	X	X	X	X	X	X
O Evaluating information	–	X	–	–	–	–	–
P Organising and presenting information	X	X	X	X	X	X	X

Source: Torrington, Weightman and Peacock, 1992

safety, economic trends, as well as technical aspects. Presentation to panel from industry. Half marks for individual effort, half for group success.

- Group Laboratory Projects (50 hours) – including a written report and a seminar.
- Case studies – provide familiarity with real situations.
- Fourth year Research Project – starts with two months on location with environmental problem, then dissertation (keeping contact with company) and presentation.

We then looked in detail at the performance criteria of each of the MCI standards to see whether the experiences offered could be mapped against them. For example, the performance criteria of unit 7 of the MCI standards for one course came out as:

Unit (7.1) requires subordinates, so students have no scope for acquiring appropriate evidence.

Examples of the criteria for unit (7.2) – maintaining relationships with one's manager – are: inform manager about progress when appropriate, clearly and in appropriate detail; seeking advice when appropriate; and avoid damaging the relationship.

Some of these criteria will be met in the relationship with the supervisor and on any placement.

The performance criteria for establishing relationships with colleagues (7.3) may be met from experience of teamwork. Including: have honest and constructive relationships, friendly behaviour, exchanging information and opinions, help and advice, don't give offence over differences of opinion, resolve conflict, honour promises.

For the rest of section (7) there is a need for subordinates and authority to meet the performance criteria so it is not appropriate for students.

Mapping is a detailed business. It requires a thorough understanding of what experiences are available and of the criteria being applied. The process of mapping is, then, comparing these two in detail. It is always worth checking you have the up-to-date criteria as they may have been changed. For example, the MCI assessment included 'workplace' assessment when the above mapping was done. This has now become 'work based' assessment, which allows simulation and is easier for educational establishments such as universities to provide.

Problems of assessment

The problems encountered in running any scheme of assessment, such as competencies and appraisal schemes, are formidable – despite constant attempts to build bigger and better schemes that cannot possibly fail. Here are a few of these problems, mostly based on experience of appraisal schemes, relevant to any assessment scheme in the workplace.

1. **Paperwork**   Systems always involve a lot of paperwork and documentation which is disliked by the managers who have to carry out the assessments. There is no escape from the documentation, however, as an essential feature of assessment is reporting, and schemes invariably include attempts to make both the judgements and the reporting consistent between different assessors. This, unavoidably, involves forms and detailed instructions.
2. **Formality**   The forms and the general paraphernalia introduce an inhibiting feature into the everyday working relationships between managers and their subordinates, who dislike

the idea of formal evaluation and prefer a more relaxed, easy-going basis to their working relationship. Performance assessment and appraisal thus become a burdensome extra to the manager. Managers usually argue that they provide regular, informal performance feedback and evaluation hour-by-hour, so that form filling is irrelevant. This conveniently ignores the benefit of thinking out a considered view of the whole working performance rather than simply pointing out errors when they occur. It also does not take account of providing the counselling and training aspects of feedback to the person assessed, which are only likely to register when there is a serious discussion about performance.

3. **Outcomes are ignored**   Managers will not stick with their judgements, so if it is agreed that person A should have six months' training elsewhere, the manager may still not find time to send that person. Promotion decisions are often inconsistent with the results of the most recent assessment, in that the most appropriate person – according to the forms – is not the one chosen for promotion. This may be due to the promotion decision being irrational, or to a need to maintain a necessary political balance by advancing someone's protégé, or to experience and judgement overriding the dictates of the system.

4. **Performance is measured by proxy**   Performance assessment is used in situations where performance cannot be readily measured, so proxies for performance are often measured instead.

> It may be difficult for me to determine if you are effective at your job; however, I can tell if you are at work on time, if you look busy, if you are pleasant and agreeable, or if you respect authority. While these characteristics may or may not have a relationship to performance, they are frequently easier to measure than performance *per se*. So, what we often find in organizations is the use of one or more proxies for performance rather than actual measures of performance. The use of proxies by managers, especially inadequate ones, can produce considerable dysfunctional behavior among employees. However, this does not stop managers from using them.
>
> Robbins (1978), p. 209

Lists of competencies are frequently used within organisations to try to overcome this problem.

5. **The just above average syndrome**   The assessment carries either an explicit or implicit statement about the general ability and acceptability of the person assessed. Designers of appraisal systems go to great lengths to force assessors to provide a range of judgements, but there is great reluctance to tell anyone that they are not doing well enough, or to put 'black marks' on paper. There is also a reluctance to tell people that they are outstanding, as this raises expectations that may not be satisfied. There is thus a tendency for most people assessed to be judged as comfortably above average. There is then no demand for remedial action by poor performers and no problem about high flyers asking for promotion. The best that this achieves is to prevent the scheme causing too much trouble: the high flyers are frustrated through lack of recognition and the under-achievers leap enthusiastically to the conclusion that they are doing just the right thing.

6. **The unwillingness of managers to face up to unpopular judgements**   Managers may be concerned that hearing the bad news will destroy the working relationship between them and the subordinate, and this unease is compounded by the preference for informality. A formal structure enables a manager to be critical. Without that structure, adverse criticism is likely to develop into recriminations and vituperation, especially when it is judgement that is being deployed rather than measurement.

7. **Incomplete coverage**   For competency schemes to be fair they have to be applied to *all* employees in a particular cadre, and for schemes to be effective they have to be *seen* to be fair. In operation, most schemes fail to achieve complete coverage. Another aspect of complete coverage being lost is in the decay of schemes. Enthusiasts with their careers at stake may succeed in bullying all colleagues to complete assessments once, or even twice, only to be succeeded by someone seeking to try assessment in a different way and gaining the approval of colleagues by leaving the existing scheme in abeyance for the time being. However, schemes only begin to pay off when they become an established part of the way the organisation functions. Altering them can be as damaging as digging up a plant to see if it is growing.

8. **Ill-informed assessors and context problems**   A prerequisite for sound assessment is knowledge by the assessor of the performance that is being assessed. Without safeguards, managers may be asked, because of their rank, to assess members of the organisation whose work they do not know. Alternatively, they may be unduly influenced by recent events which are clear in their minds. The problem of context is how one disentangles individual performance from the circumstances in which it occurs.

Despite these problems, judging people and assessing their ability to do the job is part of organisational life. The argument for using competencies as part of the assessment procedure is that they focus attention on the behaviours and performance of individuals and their ability to get things done. Of course, the assessment is not totally objective and it can certainly be time consuming. The clever thing is to try to focus resources on those competencies that really make the difference and are worth the attention, and not to waste time and energy on assessing the obvious unless there is a particular problem – if only it were as easy to do as it is to write!

References

DULEWICZ, V. (1989) Assessment Centres as the Route to Competence. *Personnel Management*, Nov.

FLETCHER, S. (1991) *NVQs Standards and Competence*, Kogan Page. London

LLOYD, C. and COOK, A. (1993) *Implementing Standards of Competence*. Kogan Page, London

ROBBINS, S. P. (1978) *Personnel: The Management of Human Resources*. Prentice Hall Englewood Cliffs, New Jersey

TORRINGTON, D., WEIGHTMAN, J. and PEACOCK, A. (1992) MCI Competence Standards and Engineering and Science Students at UMIST. Unpublished report for TEED, July

WOODRUFFE, C. (1994) *Assessment Centres*, 2nd edn, IPM, London

8

How Do You Develop Competency?

Getting action attached to the titles and lists of competency is *the* issue. Just developing a list of appropriate competencies and assessing the required ones will do little or nothing to improve the performance of individuals or the organisation. It is only by using these assessments to help individuals develop and relate to the organisation core competencies through jobs and careers that the process has any pay-off. This requires a thoughtful understanding of the individual, their competencies and the organisation.

Chapters 3 and 4 discuss several different starting points for using competency analysis. Your answers at that stage will determine, to some extent, your needs at this stage. If you are looking for a major cultural change and a focus on the organisation's core competencies then you will need a long-term development plan for the whole organisation with commensurate top management commitment. If your ambitions are somewhat smaller, such as a desire to improve recruitment, then you will need to develop those involved in the recruitment process.

Chapter 7 started with several questions to ask yourself about assessing competency in others. Within an organisation there is really very little point in spending a lot of time doing the assessment unless the results are to be used to improve the effectiveness of the individuals and the unit they work in. This chapter deals with different aspects of doing this.

Using a competencies approach is more about what needs training and developing and how to assess improvements in competency than about dictating particular ways of doing the training and developing. The distinctive feature of using competencies is in the identifying of training needs and in its evaluation where the approach is focused on listing required performance standards. It is hoped that by a careful use of competency lists and assessment that training and development programmes will be more precisely targeted rather than giving people training wholesale, because it is thought to be good for them. If this careful targeting is to be effective, some careful consideration of what would be the most cost-effective way of achieving the improved competency also needs to be given. As elsewhere in the book, I have not given you 'right answers' but hope to give you sufficient information and analysis for you to think of what would be appropriate to *your* specific situation. Particularly, I have included a list of different approaches to training and development, which are by no means specific to using a competencies approach, to spark you into thinking of which way would be best to develop a particular competency. If you know *what* you are trying to train or develop it is rather easier to select a method because it is useful than when there is only a vague idea that the performance needs to be improved. This book is about using a competency approach; a wider ranging book on identifying training needs is Bee and Bee (1994).

Managing people

Using a competency approach requires a much more hands-on involvement with each other than has sometimes been the tradition for managers and staff. You can hardly talk, assess and develop competencies without getting down to nitty gritty discussions about what is meant by the terms and how they fit the minutiae of the business. This sort of discussion fits in ideologically with other current management ideas such as human resource management, quality management and the ideas about empowerment. All these movements emphasise managers really managing people by getting involved with the people who work for them and understanding what is preventing them from performing better. This book is not a general book on managing people so if you want to read further about these issues you could try Torrington and Weightman (1994) or Honey (1988).

The real strength of the competency aspect of this style of managing people is the emphasis on the learning which could take place. As Fletcher says:

> 'Competency-based appraisal does allow some scope for comparing people, but its real strength is in analysing the progress of the individual and in directing attention to those areas where skills

can be improved. It is developmentally orientated, and as such is likely to be motivating for the person appraised . . . and is more concerned with the medium and longer term than with the next 6–12 months.'

Fletcher (1993), p. 33

Mumford (1993) takes the discussion further by pointing out that the competency approach, with its emphasis on applied prior learning, will require successful intervention by bosses that has not yet been seriously tackled by organisations. The use of competencies shows there is a need for self development, organisation development and boss-derived development. In Mumford's view, these can be met by encouraging a use of the learning opportunities which come up in the normal working environment rather than by contriving special activities for development. He suggests the following opportunities could be used for learning:

Meetings
Customer visits
Specific tasks
Visit to plant or office
Managing a change
Social occasions
Foreign travel
Charity and sports clubs
Reading
Walking the floor

Mumford (1993)

The important point is that bosses need to be aware of these and any other opportunities and to think where the competency of individuals can be developed in the normal workplace so that they are ready for the future.

Managing the process

As well as managing some of the learning that is available to individuals, managers will also have to manage other issues to do with the use of competencies. The 'Questions to ask yourself' section at the beginning of Chapter 7 gives some of these issues. Decisions about who sees the assessments and the use to which assessments can be put involve important cultural messages; how these decisions are taken also involves important cultural messages. Do we emphasise the rights of the individual to control the use and who sees the assessments or do we emphasise the right of the organisation as a whole to use the outcomes for the interest of all? Where there is a lot of suspicion and mistrust in organisations there tends to be an emphasis on the need for managers to control. Similarly, organisations which genuinely work as teams, with high levels of trust, also leave managers to control procedures as they feel that it is not an issue. In between tend to be organisations which emphasise the rights of individuals. The important management message is to take decisions about these issues which suit the particular circumstances and culture of the organisation.

Another important issue which needs careful thought is that of who is to monitor the outcomes of the assessment process and how it should be done. This process could be done by individuals, line managers, the personnel department or managing director. The advantages of the individual doing so are they are responsible for their own development and can be very motivated by the process. The disadvantage is that not all will do it and most will not have the clout to demand the necessary resources for change. The advantage of the line manager doing it is they are involved directly with the individual and have more organisational clout to get things done. The advantage of the personnel department doing it is they can coordinate across the organisation so there is not duplication. Finally, the advantage of the MD doing the monitoring is that he or she will then know where everyone is up to, but this is really only feasible where the organisation is sufficiently small, say less than 200 staff.

Further questions are, 'Should assessments be compulsory or just for those who want to develop' and 'Who is responsible for negotiating the resource implications for any changes which are suggested?' Again, the answers to these will be contingent on the style of management of any particular unit or organisation. Centrally controlled compulsory assessment and negotiation of resources will fit the ordered, planned organisation. The self-selecting assessment and self-managed negotiation of resources suits the loosely coupled organisation. Knowing which to emphasise in your particular setting, which may change from time to time, is the art of management.

Continuous development

Continuous development is currently being widely advocated as a way of coping with rapid changes. It is about encouraging learning at all times. The argument is that the more an individual learns, the more confident they become at doing so – they learn to learn, and are likely to want to learn some more. Reid et al. (1992) summarise the process in a continuous development spiral (see Figure 8.1). This learning can take place in all sorts of settings – both formal and informal – not necessarily only in formal training sessions. Looking at Mumford's list, one can see that the active learner could maximise their skills and understanding of the organisation, whereas the timid would concentrate merely on their own current performance. The list was compiled for managers but could equally well apply to others who are not called managers. It might be useful to get individuals to take this list and then develop a personal list of learning opportunities in their own life, at work and/or home.

Training

The argument that the best way of dealing with the demand for constant change is to become an active learner has led to an increasing emphasis at work on training, as we saw in Chapter 2. Where there are professional trainers involved, there is likely to be an emphasis on systematic training. This approach has an inbuilt logic to it, is advocated by the Department of Employment and is called the systematic training cycle. In this approach identifying what needs training is carefully analysed before the training is planned; carrying out the training and then evaluating the whole process completes the cycle. This approach clearly fits the use of competencies as they can be used for identifying the training needs and evaluating any improved performance afterwards. This cycle requires time and careful monitoring so presumes, in practice, a training specialist or department to carry it out.

The two important considerations for training and development, whichever approach one chooses, are first, how do we decide what to train and develop and second, how should we go about doing the training and developing.

Figure 8.1
The Continuous Development Spiral

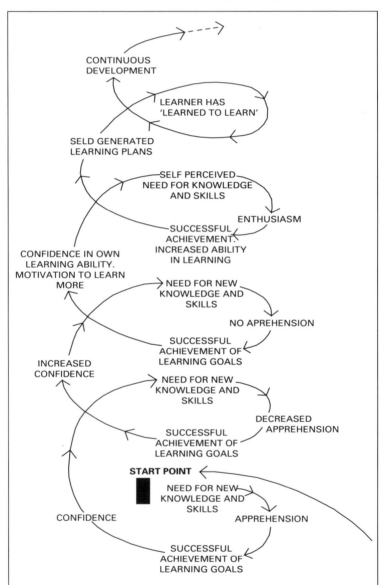

CONTINUOUS
DEVELOPMENT

LEARNER HAS
'LEARNED TO LEARN'

SELD GENERATED
LEARNING PLANS

SELF PERCEIVED
NEED FOR KNOWLEDGE
AND SKILLS

ENTHUSIASM

SUCCESSFUL
ACHIEVEMENT.
INCREASED ABILITY
IN LEARNING

CONFIDENCE IN OWN
LEARNING ABILITY.
MOTIVATION TO LEARN
MORE

NEED FOR NEW
KNOWLEDGE AND
SKILLS

NO APREHENSION

SUCCESSFUL
ACHIEVEMENT OF
LEARNING GOALS

INCREASED
CONFIDENCE

NEED FOR NEW
KNOWLEDGE AND
SKILLS

DECREASED
APPREHENSION

SUCCESSFUL
ACHIEVEMENT OF
LEARNING GOALS

START POINT

NEED FOR NEW
KNOWLEDGE AND
SKILLS

CONFIDENCE

APPREHENSION

SUCCESSFUL
ACHIEVEMENT OF
LEARNING GOALS

Source: Reid et al., 1992

130

Deciding what to train and develop

If we see training and developing as the process of bringing someone to a level of competency, we have to know what is required. In most large organisations there is a training department or training officer who has the organisational responsibility for this sort of activity and most managers need have no more than a passing understanding of the process that is involved. In smaller organisations, where managers have to manage everything, help can be available from TECs, colleges and employers' organisations for this sort of activity.

In a simple management-led training programme there may be some sequence resembling the following one.

- The manager will want the employee to understand the task to be performed and to be able to do what is required at a reasonable level of competency. There then needs to be some assessment of whether there is a gap in competency between the job which needs doing and the job holder.
- A comparison is made between the job analysis and the individual analysis and the difference will lead to a diagnosis of training need. This gap becomes the training aims and objectives. It may be that new techniques are being introduced; it may be that old skills have faded or that there has never been sufficient understanding to do the job superbly.
- If the difference between performance required and performance given is too wide, aspects of managing poor performance will need to be invoked. These involve analysing the reasons behind the poor performance. There may be personal reasons outside the organisation's control, organisational reasons outside the individual's control, or a mismatch between the two. Having established the reason, it is easier to see possible strategies for dealing with the poor performance. See Video Arts (1984) for a delightful video and book about this problem.

This systematic approach to identifying training needs is now widely accepted in training departments but it should always be remembered that the whole process is dependent on judgement at various points and so, appropriately, should involve managers outside the training department. For a fuller discussion of this whole issue, see Bee and Bee (1994).

Training and development methods

Once the training need is identified, it is time to consider developing and training to meet these needs. This does not necessarily mean a formal training experience. Looking at Mumford's list (p. 127) may give you some ideas of how to develop; others are given below.

Recent preoccupation with training methods may have led some people to conclude that training would be effective provided the correct method was selected for a given application. There can, however, be too great a concern about method at the expense of substance. A study, conducted among 64 students taught by different modes and tested both immediately after the teaching session and again one month later, showed no difference in the results achieved by lecturing, case studies and role play or other experiential methods. This study came up with the conclusion:

> 'It appears trainees can learn effectively in a variety of modes, perhaps indeed finding as much or more satisfaction from what they are learning than the way in which they are trained.'
>
> Gale et al. (1982) p. 16

Despite this cautionary note, the method of training and development still has to be appropriate for the purpose to be served. Here is a brief description, in alphabetical order, of some of the more common methods of training and developing competencies with some of the associated advantages and disadvantages. They are listed here as a starting point for you to look through when you want to develop your own or someone else's competencies. I have tried to give a brief, real example for each to give some flavour of the different methods.

Acting up   Acting up is doing a more senior job temporarily to cover for absence or vacancy, for example maternity cover. An individual can broaden their experience and skill within a position of greater responsibility.

An example is the head of a sixth form acting up as a deputy headteacher when the deputy is on secondment as head to a neighbouring school, due for amalgamation with yet another school in nine months' time.

Action learning   This involves the linking of a structured task and action within the learning process using action learning sets. These are groups of people who discuss the problems with an identified facilitator. It can be difficult to keep the group on the task and complete the task as individuals develop, but it is found particularly useful by chief executives who enjoy being part of a group as they can feel very isolated.

One group was made up of six personnel directors from two regional health authorities who came together to develop a personnel auditing form. They originally met on a course but continued meeting infrequently for two years after, with a facilitator, to complete the task.

Audio visual presentations   These include slides, films and videos, with videos being far the most common. This technique is similar to a lecture in what it can achieve, but video has an additional advantage over a lecture in that you can stop and start it as you want.

The Video Arts film mentioned above (Video Arts, 1984) is a good example.

Case study   This is where a history of some event is given and the trainees are invited to analyse the causes of a problem or to find a solution. This provides an opportunity for a cool look at problems and for the exchange of ideas about possible solutions. However, trainees may not realise that the real world is not quite the same as the training session.

MBA students are given lots of these, to study various business problems. One such might be the position of British supermarkets faced with low cost competition from abroad in the early 1990s. What should they do about it?

Coaching   This is improving the performance of someone who is already competent rather than establishing competency in the first place. Further aspects of coaching are: it is usually on a one-to-one basis, is set in the everyday working situation and is a continuing activity. It is gently nudging people to improve their performance, to develop their skills and to increase their self-confidence so that they can take more responsibility for their own work and develop their career prospects. Most coaching is done by people with their own subordinates, but the subordinate position of the person coached is by no means a prerequisite. What is essential is that the coach should have the qualities of expertise, judgement and experience that make it possible for the person being coached to follow the guidance.

A personal example is the coaching my colleague Derek Torrington has given me over the past 14 years in the writing of management texts. It happens less often now than it did!

Delegation   Delegation is not giving people jobs to do – it is giving people scope, responsibility and authority. It allows individuals to test their own ideas, develop understanding and confidence, and flex some muscles. The more specific the instructions and terms of reference, the less learning will be managed as a result of that activity. With the assignment delegated, the individual then starts work on his or her own initiative. The decision when to seek guidance and discussion on progress from the manager is also theirs, so that action is always in their own hands.

When a senior sales manager hands over a portfolio of customers to a junior this would be called delegation if the junior is given the autonomy to decide how to work with these customers.

Discussion   This is where knowledge, ideas and opinions on a subject are exchanged between trainees and trainer. This is particularly suitable where the application is a matter of opinion, for changing attitudes and finding out how knowledge is going to be applied. The technique requires skill on the part of the trainer as it can be difficult to keep discussion focused and useful.

This example involves section managers of a department store which was introducing performance appraisal for the first time. At the end of the day of training, which included talks and role play, there was a general discussion about performance appraisal and deciding how to go forward with an action plan. It was run with both the trainer and the senior manager present.

Distance learning This method involves the individual utilising a range of teaching materials outside the traditional course environment. It is self learning and requires high levels of personal discipline, but it can be difficult to sustain in isolation.

The Open University and Linguaphone language courses are probably the most well known examples.

Exercise In an exercise trainees do a particular task, in a particular way, to get a particular result. This is suitable when trainees need practice in following a procedure or formula to reach a required objective. The exercise must be realistic.

Most of us have had to do exercises to master the latest technology such as using the PC, fax, answerphone or video.

Group dynamics Using this method, trainees are put into situations where the behaviour of the individuals and the group is examined. The task given to the group usually requires them to cooperate before they can achieve the objective. Observers collect information about how the trainees go about this and then feedback to the group and individuals after the task is completed. Trainees learn about the effect they have on others. This may be threatening and anxieties need to be resolved before the end of the session. This is very dependent on the quality of the trainer and can be dangerous if entered into too casually. Usually the task is relatively remote from work.

An example of this method is of local authority computer staff on a communications course who were asked to build a tower from straws. The tower was then judged on height, robustness and artistic merit. Other tasks used for this sort of development experience are trying to build a bridge from logs which will not quite reach across a stream or prioritising the materials to be moved after an imaginary air crash.

Job rotation In job rotation individuals do different jobs within the section or organisation over a period of time. By setting up flexible working patterns within the organisation, individuals can be facilitated to broaden their experience and skills.

The operators on a chemical plant, for example, work on all parts of the plant – from managing the raw materials, making the material, taking samples for quality control, to checking the final packing and labelling.

Learning contracts   These are usually agreed between an individual, their boss, and whoever is providing the learning experience. They specify what learning opportunities are expected, when these will occur and what outcomes are expected. The aim is to ensure everyone agrees and the individual is then expected to monitor their own performance against this contract. Contracts can also be used in conjunction with informal learning and to generate learning opportunities at work.

Third year psychology students going out to employers on work experience had a contract agreed between the student, the employers and the psychology tutor.

Lecture   A lecture is a talk given without much participation by the trainees. The method is suitable for large audiences where the information to be got over can be worked out precisely in advance. There is little opportunity for feedback, so some in the audience may not get the point. It requires careful preparation and should never be longer than forty minutes.

A lecture on competencies to second year management students at a university is an obvious example.

On the job   With this method, trainees work in the real environment with support from a skilled person. This gives the trainee real practice and it does not involve expensive new equipment. However, not all skilled people are skilled trainers. The essential ingredients are briefing, feedback and support that help the individual to achieve the objectives in a structured way.

A new business manager was in the office for two weeks before the old business manager moved to a new job. This overlap meant a smooth handover of procedures and commitments, and provided an example of on-the-job training.

Programmed instruction   Programmed instruction is also called computer assisted learning (CAL). Trainees work at their own pace using a book or computer programme which has a series of tasks and tests geared to teaching something systematically. It is suitable for learning logical skills and knowledge. However, it does not allow discussion with others which may be important where the application could be debatable.

Many institutions have such programmes about how to use

their services, for example libraries and Training and Enterprise Councils (TECs).

Project Similar to an exercise, a project allows greater freedom to display initiative and creative ideas. Projects provide feedback on a range of personal qualities. They need the full interest and cooperation of the trainee and specific terms of reference.

Figure 8.2 was the outcome of a brief project given to a group of four people on a week-long innovation and creativity course in London organised for a large multinational organisation. The project was to develop a game which the other members of the course could play next day. Obviously, projects can be much bigger and more realistic than this. The members of this group felt they had learned a lot about putting some of the techniques learned on the course into practice.

Figure 8.2
A brief project

LOST – LOndon Sightseeing Trip
The objective of the game is to see some of the sights of London and do this faster than your opponent.

Rules of the game:
Start and end point of the journey is Heathrow Airport, Terminal 4.

The only means of transport is the Underground. You can move on the Underground system by throwing the dice; the number of dice represent the number of stops you can go. Travel in any one go is in any direction you like – switching lines whenever, wherever you like.

While travelling, you may encounter some attractions/sights of London. These are marked on the board. Each sight/attraction has been giving a points value. You will have to have collected at least . . . points before you can return to Heathrow. At each sight, you will have to answer a question as on the QUESTION cards. Upon successful answering of the question, you will receive a token to state that you have 'done' the sight.

> If you fail to answer a question correctly, you lose your turn and your opponent is next; you will not collect a token.
>
> A sight can only be visited once; if you happen to arrive at a sight after you have collected a token for it, you will not be eligible for another token for that sight.
>
> The winner of the game is the first one to arrive back at Terminal 4 having collected the required amount of points.

Role play   In this training method, trainees are asked to act the role they, or someone else, would play at work. It is used particularly for face-to-face situations and is suitable for near to real life work, where criticism would be useful. The difficulties are that trainees can be embarrassed and the usefulness is very dependent on the quality of the feedback.

In the appraisal training in the department store (see 'Discussion' above) the participants practised interviewing each other using different techniques. Then they role played by conducting a mini appraisal interview about each other's work over the previous week.

Secondment   This involves organising a placement in an alternative department or organisation for the achievement of a specific goal. It is often used for management and professional development. The individual may, of course, choose not to come back!

One evening two people relaxing in the pub thought it would be fun to swap jobs for three months. Each of them saw their boss the next morning and, to their astonishment, both bosses thought it an excellent idea (the bosses also knew both the participants). Two months later a university researcher and a teacher trainer, in separate insitutions, swapped jobs for a term. They both learned a lot and held extraordinarily detailed feedback conversations with each other about the work.

Simulation   This training method involved the use of a mock up of a real life situation/equipment to give people experience before they encounter the real thing. It can be used for initial training, updating, keeping in practice or introducing new techniques. The expense of creating a realistic mock up is really only justified where practising on the real thing is totally impossible or would be catastrophic if there happened to be a mistake.

Flight simulators for air pilots, mock battles for the military and practice on cadavers for surgeons are dramatic examples. But the increasing sophistication of computer graphics have enabled all sorts of simulations and 'virtual reality' to be created for workplace training and development to take place.

Skill instruction   The trainee is here told how to do it, shown how to do it, and then does it under supervision. This is suitable for putting across skills as long as the task is broken into suitable parts. What is considered suitable parts will vary with the task and the person to receive the training. This form of training is not appropriate for all skills as some tasks are best learned as a whole.

Any of the mechanical skills would be a good example here, such as a garage mechanic learning how to change an exhaust on a new model of car.

Talk   A talk allows participation by the trainees, by asking questions of them or by them. It is useful for getting over a new way of looking at things which involves some abstraction, for example some management ideas or a view of the future, and is appropriate for giving information to up to 20 people. It can only work where people are willing or able to participate. Where people do not want to participate it becomes a lecture.

When management consultants report their findings to the senior management team they often start by giving a presentation, or talk, where individuals can ask questions and test out their understanding of the findings.

Feedback

For many of the training methods listed above, the importance of the quality of feedback is critical to the success of the learning. Every person developing others has to provide feedback, so that the trainee can compare their performance with the required standard and can see the progress being made. The characteristics of good feedback are immediacy and precision. If feedback comes immediately after the action, the trainee has the best chance of associating an error with that part of the performance that caused it, whereas delay will emphasise what was wrong, but the memory of what happened will have faded. Precision in feedback requires the information conveyed to be as accurate as possible and related to what the trainee has done, rather than the results of this action, so that the trainee is able to pinpoint the action that needs to be remedied and how it can be altered. In teaching someone to drive a car, you may well have the alarming experience of the car lurching forward from a stationary position and then stopping dead. The comment to the trainee driver 'not smooth enough' is unhelpful as it makes an obvious statement about what the car has done instead of explaining what the driver did wrong. 'Too quick on the clutch' focuses on what the driver did, but in language that will probably be imprecise to the listener. Something like 'You brought the clutch pedal up too quickly with the left foot' would be precise feedback.

Part of the feedback process is giving reinforcement and is very important. This is praising and underpinning satisfactory performance by encouraging trainees with plenty of positive comment and reward – like giving lumps of sugar to a well-behaved horse. Apparently, if you put people into a room to find something and reward them every time they get nearer the object, as in the child's game 'getting warmer', they find the object quickly. That is, they learn. Alternatively, if you punish them every time they go in the wrong direction they come to a complete halt and never find the object. That is, they do not learn. One estimate is that people learn quickest with 80 per cent positive experiences.

Although this is a useful general rule, it is not a complete explanation of how people learn:

> 'Learning is not fundamentally a matter of gradually strengthening connections but rather an all-or-none event. Thus most modern theorists tend to favour the idea that the individual connection is acquired on a single occasion . . . The effects of repetition may be to recruit more and more single connections, but each one is learned or not learned.'
>
> Gagne (1975), p. 44

Organisation development

So far we have emphasised the development of individual competencies and the differing ways of doing this. Another equally
important way of developing competency in organisations, and
individuals, comes through organisation development. There are
literally dozens of ways of doing this but all are aimed at making
the organisation more effective and competent. It may be done
through a comprehensive human resources management (HRM)
approach, through a decisive development of a particular corporate culture, or some strategic initative. This book is not about
organisation development but you could look at Williams et al.
(1993). Any systematic attempt to reorganise is likely to have as
part of the brief the development of staff, to develop their competency to work in the new 'developed' organisation. This could
well use the competency approach we have discussed in this
book.

Careers

Another aspect of developing competency is developing careers
over a long period of time. This may be developing our own
career within one or several organisations or managing others'
careers within the organisation.

Managers have to learn how to manage talent and this includes
developing staff so that they build careers to suit themselves.
This is increasingly important if Kanter's comments about security of employment coming from being employable rather than
from being employed (see Chapter 2) are true. All of us need
opportunities to develop skills and a reputation. This involves
ensuring that subordinates get a variety of opportunities and
experiences as well as being assessed. As Handy puts it, managers have to be 'teacher, counsellor and friend, as much or more
than he or she is commander, inspector and judge' (Handy, 1989,
p. 104).

My colleague Valmai Bowden, looking at the careers of bench
scientists, has pointed out that this nurturing of people's careers
can be compared to parenting. Some managers are very strict
and dogmatic – 'do it like me' – others are more facilitating and

encourage self-direction and assessment. Those who are lucky enough to have good 'parenting' are likely to develop into the confident, learning, self-developing individuals who are more likely to have rewarding careers. Those who feel ignored and rejected can become embittered.

Most managers now realise that they must also take responsibility for their own careers. As Stewart (1991, p. 193) points out, managers' careers look very different now from the traditional progress up the ladder. The important issues are getting relevant experience and ensuring the c.v. will look good to other employers. This may be achieved by changing jobs within an organisation or between organisations.

The changes which have occurred in jobs and careers in the eighties and nineties have had major implications for individuals. Rosemary Stewart (1991, pp. 196–201) suggests the following advantages and disadvantages of these changes.

Advantages

Changes in jobs –
    More responsibility and autonomy

Changes in careers
    More control of your destiny
    A better match for one's abilities
    More variety and interest
    More flexibility in the pattern of work
    More choice of working environment

Disadvantages

Harder work and greater pressure
Less security
Less opportunity for promotion
Loneliness
Problems of dual careers

Inevitably individuals will respond to these changes in a variety of ways, but it is quite likely that more people will try to balance their life between work and home differently than in the past. This is partly because of the increased number of women working but also because of the restructuring of careers. Scase and Goffee (1989) explore how middle managers were managing their careers and give detailed descriptions of how many are reluctant managers.

The interesting thing, from our point of view, is that any personally managed career is likely to depend on demonstrable competency rather than just a network of contacts or 'waiting for Buggin's turn'.

References

BEE, F. and BEE, R. (1994) *Training Need Analysis and Evaluation*, IPM, London

FLETCHER, C. (1993) *Appraisal*, IPM, London

Gagne, R. M. (1975) *Essentials of Learning for Instruction*, Holt, Rinehart & Winston, New York

GALE, J., DAS, H. and MINER, R. (1982) Training Methods Compared, *Leadership and Organisation Behaviour Journal*, **3**, (3), 13–17

HANDY, C. (1989) *The Age of Unreason*, Business Books, London

HONEY, P. (1988) *Improve Your People Skills*, IPM, London

MUMFORD, A. (1993) How Managers Can Become Developers, *Personnel Management*, June, 42–5

REID, M. A., BARRINGTON, H. and KENNEY, J. (1992) *Training Interventions: Managing Employee Development*, 3rd edn, IPM, London

SCASE, R. and GOFFEE, R. (1989) *Reluctant Managers: Their Work and Lifestyles*, Unwin Hyman, London

STEWART, R. (1991) *Managing Today and Tomorrow*, Macmillan, Basingstoke

TORRINGTON, D. and WEIGHTMAN, J. (1994) *Effective Management*, 2nd edn, Prentice Hall, Hemel Hempstead

Video Arts (1984) *So You Think You Can Manage?*, Methuen, London

WILLIAMS, A., DOBSON, P. and WALTERS, M. (1993) *Changing Culture: New Organisational Approaches*, 2nd edn, IPM, London

9

What Else Do I Need to Consider?

In the previous chapters we have examined the questions that need to be considered and the various processes that are required to use competencies for a variety of purposes. But to improve the chance of a project being successful it is worth spending some time thinking, before you start, about how best to introduce the project and maintain it. It is usually worth having a good think through beforehand rather than rushing ahead with the project. This is not always easy to do, especially in the current climate of frantic activity and everyone 'being busy'. Where the project is a large organisation-wide initiative it may be worth taking a week away from the workplace to have a clear think about the project as a whole and how to implement it.

This short chapter is not specifically about competencies. It is intended to help you get going. I hope by now that you feel that using a competencies approach is about focusing on the behaviours that are really appropriate to the situation. With this in mind, it would seem absurd to write a practical book on competencies without including something to assist your competency in putting into practice what you have read.

Questions to ask yourself

Who do I need to influence?
– whose support is crucial?
– whose help is essential?
– who needs to be consulted?
– who is going to be involved?

What is the best way of doing this?

What timing would be most suitable?
– when would be appropriate to start this process?
– what resources are needed?
– what timetable for deciding the competencies, assessing and developing them do we have in mind?

144

> Do we have an action plan?
> – what are likely to be the major difficulties of implementing this?
> – how are we going to deal with any unexpected consequences?

Let us look at these questions before going on to other general issues which need considering before introducing competencies into the organisation.

Who do I need to influence?

Getting any innovation into practice requires championing the project through a series of meetings and people. Regardless of the scale of the project envisaged, the competencies' champion will need to define the project clearly and be sufficiently enthusiastic to persuade others. Burgelman and Sayles (1988) describe this process as 'Internal Corporate Venturing'. In their view, the process begins with technically trained, entrepreneurially inclined managers performing two linking tasks. First, new items of knowledge are linked with solving a proven need – in our case using the competencies model to solve problems such as those described in Chapters 3 and 4. This leads to the second task, championing the idea, which at successive stages involves more senior staff who are largely reactive but control the whole process by focusing on the main business rather than agreeing to too many diversions. Their model then shows how the various parts of the organisation have a role to play in getting an innovation developed.

The most obvious answer to the question, 'who do I need to influence?' would be to get the support of senior staff. Getting someone with clout to support the idea in meetings and discussions will help the process along. The larger the project, the more senior the support will need to be. If the initiative is envisaged as organisation-wide, you will need the support of the chief executive. The more enthusiastic and whole hearted this support, the more likely it is that others will listen.

You will also need the practical help of others to develop and implement the ideas. It is very useful to have a small group or working party to develop the ideas and to criticise proposals before they are exposed to those less committed to the project. This group can be made up of specialists where such people exist, usually in large organisations, such as personnel and training people. It could also be a working party of interested representatives from the groups likely to be affected. This has the advantage of at least having them committed to *trying* to make any scheme work.

You might also want to seek the help of outsiders who are specialists in the area, such as consultants, people from the local higher or further education institutions, or people from the local TEC. As with any use of consultants, it is important that you keep control of the project by managing the process. The clearer the brief received by outsiders, the more able they will be to offer appropriate help.

Where the competencies project is going to affect people in their work it is worth consulting with them before the implementation stage. It is one of the truisms of management that the more people have been involved in a process the more likely they are to try to make it work, and the less they have been involved the more likely they are to find fault. Obviously some sense of proportion has to be kept here relative to the scale of the project. Possible people to consult with are: employees, managers, trade unions, external validating bodies, and further and higher education institutions.

The nature of the consultation can be anything from a strictly informing 'tell and sell' mode to involving people and letting them take the decision. Figure 9.1 demonstrates the interaction between the amount of employee involvement and management control. It is important to choose the level normal for the particular organisation, otherwise everyone will wonder what on earth is going on.

Questions to ask yourself

Who else do you need to influence before the project gets going?

Is there anyone who is going to be involved in the project who has not been contacted?

Who else needs to be informed about the proposals?

Figure 9.1
Participation: the interaction between employee involvement and management control

Participation

How one implements change will vary with the type of participation that is practised in the organisation or department. In some the convention will be that there is extensive consultation to win consent for what is proposed; in others change will be implemented by decree. The figure below lists categories of consent sought in different organisations before implementing change.

Category of employee consent

1 Controlling When there is employee control, as in a cooperative, managers are authorized to act by the employees.

2 Participative Employees do not control the business, but participate in decision-making on major issues.

3 Negotiated Employees limit the freedom of managers to introduce change through the separation of some matters on which action can be based only on some form of mutual accommodation.

4 Consultative Managers ask for the opinions of employees before implementing change, although the opinions may be partly or completely ignored.

5 Grudging Where managers are not willing to consult on decisions, or where unions are not strong enough to require consultation, there will be no explicit challenge from employees, but this does not necessarily mean commitment.

6 Normative In some organisations there is a strong sense of moral obligation to the leadership which is engendered among the employees. Any challenge or questioning would be unthinkable as it would imply a refutation of the shared values, or norms.

Increasing degree of employee involvement and decreasing degree of management power

Decreasing degree of employee involvement and increasing degree of management power

Source: Torrington and Weightman, 1991

147

What timing would be most suitable?

There is absolutely no point in initiating a competencies project when there are other major reorganisations going on, unless the competencies project is part of that reorganisation. It is unlikely that you will ever find a moment when nothing is going on but competency-based projects are perhaps easiest to develop when they are seen as a solution to a problem which is already receiving attention. Chapters 3 and 4 suggested some reasons why you might have decided to get involved with competencies. A realistic timetable for this must involve time to budget for the necessary resources. This means fitting in with budgeting cycles and may involve settling for pump priming money the first year to set things up and a major commitment of time and money in the second or third year for training and development. You will also need to budget for time and resources at the end, to deal with the inevitable unexpected consequences which accompany any change. Certainly, many people I have talked to about their experience of introducing competencies have said that it takes more commitment and a longer time than was first thought.

Cultural and gender issues

A special issue which needs thinking about before going too far with the proposed project is that of culture and gender. All organisations, and their managers, need to be aware of cultural and gender bias which may be implicit in their procedures. The equal opportunities legislation, such as the Equal Pay Act 1970, the Sex Discrimination Act 1975 and the Race Relations Act 1976, are designed to stop discrimination in the terms and working conditions available to people. The legislation is usually interpreted to mean equal value for equal worth. This has occasionally been overinterpreted and has led to the apparent nonsenses that the tabloid press takes delight in reporting. However, the underlying issue of treating people equally and fairly is a very strong belief in the Western democracies, and organisations need to be seen to be doing this if they want employees to trust managers and work willingly in the interests of the organisation.

The areas where discrimination most commonly occurs are job

advertisements, recruitment procedures, promotion, training and transfer policies. By using a more systematic approach to these areas of human resources procedures there is a better chance of reducing discrimination. This will assist compliance with the equal opportunities legislation and improve the perceived fairness of the procedures. The competencies approach is particularly useful in this context as it concentrates on what is needed and what people can actually do, regardless of gender, nationality, religion, disability or race.

However, great care has to be taken that the required competencies are defined in a suitably non-discriminatory way. Where the analysis is based on functional analysis, that is an output-based list, it is important to ensure the list really is about desired outcomes. Where the list is input generated, that is an analysis of the general qualities which enable the appropriate behaviours to take place, it is even more important to be vigilant to prevent possible inappropriate discriminatory statements creeping in.

Questions to ask yourself

Does this competency have to be done in a particular way?

Can it be done in a variety of other ways equally satisfactorily?

Have we defined the competencies in such a way that it would be difficult for some people to ever demonstrate competency here? For example:
- have we included unnecessary strength or height requirements?
- have we included unnecessary constraints which might offend particular religious beliefs?
- have we done the analysis and drawn the list up using people who have done this in the past?
- could other people do it differently but equally satisfactorily?

Does the assessment procedure unfairly favour one group over another?

Perhaps the simplest question to ask yourself is, does this competency as written and assessed preclude anyone from doing it for reasons other than competency?

Using competencies is about discriminating between people. The purpose is to discriminate on the basis of their competency to do the job not on the basis of their gender, race, beliefs or nationality. Every step of the development and use of the competencies needs to be monitored to ensure that this is the case.

Another similar consideration in drawing up the list of competencies is the international dimension. The competencies, and the way they are to be assessed, need to consider the range of nationalities who may use them. In multinational organisations there is a need to ensure competency statements will be understood in similar terms throughout the world. For smaller organisations operating in the UK there is an increasing need to ensure that they think in European terms. For example, one chemical company now sets European-wide marketing competencies which are used for the annual performance appraisal throughout its European organisation. When using competencies it makes sense to ensure that they can be used in as wide a geographical area as possible.

Figure 9.2
Force field analysis

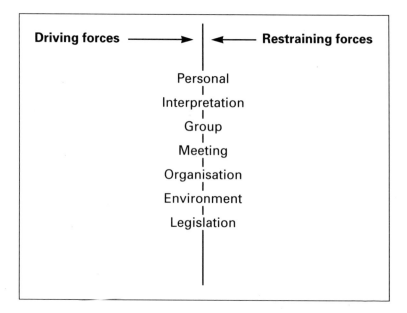

Do we have an action plan?

Action plans are simple plans to try to get things to actually happen. They are relatively short term and seek to prioritise the actions necessary to implement something. This includes a statement of the goal, an assessment of the present position, how far from the goal this is, what resources are available, what will help to achieve the goal and what will hinder the achievement of the goal. One way of systematising these thoughts is to use force field analysis (see Figure 9.2). The list in the middle of Figure 9.2 is a starting point listing different areas to think about, but you may well have others.

Action plans are sometimes called goal planning and involve setting objectives. Objectives are specific parts of the process that need to be met to achieve the goal. They are the detailed strategies and tasks that are the means by which the end is achieved. The objectives are most usefully thought out and expressed in specific statements so it is clear when they are done. Figures 9.3 and 9.4 are two goal-planning forms for going through this process. They are generally most usefully employed when other strategies are not working and for introducing new methods such as competencies.

All change has unexpected consequences and we have to deal with them. Indeed, one of the main tasks of operations managers and many middle managers in large organisations is to deal with the difference between plan and reality. One of the most useful attitudes to have is one of tolerance that things have not worked out quite as planned and acceptance that it will take slightly longer than expected. Allowance for this should be made in allocating resources.

So now all that is left to do is to stop reading and have a go at competencies, however competently!

References

BURGELMAN, R. A. and SAYLES, L. R. (1988) *Inside Corporate Innovation – Strategy, Structure and Managerial Skills*, The Free Press, New York

TORRINGTON, D. and WEIGHTMAN, J. (1991) *Action Management*, IPM, London

Figure 9.3
A goal-planning form

Goal planning
1. Decide what your goal is. Write it down with the criteria you will use to judge whether the goal has been met.
2. List the strengths you have already that will help you achieve the goal. Examples of the areas you might think about are given below.
3. List what you still need to reach your goal. Write these as concretely as possible so you can tell when you have met the need and it has become a strength. The same list as the strengths might help you to think about all the areas.
4. If a need is particularly difficult to achieve use the form in Figure 9.4 to break the need into smaller, more easily achieved objectives.

Goal	
Strengths	Needs
1 Time 2 Place 3 Money 4 Materials 5 Cooperation of . . . 6 Agreement of . . . 7 Expertise 8 9 10	

Source: Torrington and Weightman, 1991

Figure 9.4

A goal-planning form for setting objectives

Setting objectives

1. Objectives can be to meet goals set by oneself or others.

2. Make a list of the various possible ways of achieving the goal. Asking others for their ideas may increase your list of options but they are likely to be disappointed if their idea is not used.

3. Decide which is the most appropriate method by comparing the advantages and disadvantages of each.

4. The goal-planning form in Figure 9.3 can be used to establish the strengths and needs of reaching the goal in this way.

5. When dividing the needs into specific objectives it is advisable to state them so that an answer 'yes, that is done', can be given or not. Deadlines help the constantly-interrupted manager.

Need

	Objective	Method	Target date	Date done
1				
2				
3				
4				
5				
6				

Source: Torrington and Weightman, 1991

153

Index

With nearly 100,000 members, the **Institute of Personnel and Development** is the largest organisation in Europe dealing with the management and development of people. The IPD operates its own publishing unit, producing books and research reports for human resource practitioners, students, and general managers charged with people management responsibilities.

Currently there are some 160 titles covering the full range of personnel and development issues. The books have been commissioned from leading experts in the field and are packed with the latest information and guidance to best practice.

For free copies of the IPD Books Catalogue, please contact the publishing department:

Tel.: 020-8263 3387
Fax: 020-8263 3850
E-mail: publish@ipd.co.uk
Web: www.ipd.co.uk

Orders for books should be sent to:

Plymbridge Distributors
Estover
Plymouth
Devon
PL6 7PZ

(Credit card orders) Tel.: 01752 202 301
Fax: 01752 202 333

Everyone Needs a Mentor: Fostering talent at work
David Clutterbuck

Second edition

This popular book looks at how mentoring works, the benefits for both the individual and the company, the selection of mentors and mentees, and the ways of introducing and managing the formal programme.

An excellent book that ought to be purchased even by those who have the first edition – illuminating and persuasive

Alan Mumford, Industrial and Commercial Training

1993   128 pages   ISBN 0 85292 461 5   **£10.95**

Job Analysis: A manager's guide
Michael Pearn and Rajvinder Kandola

Second edition

A series of invaluable techniques for assessing how work is done – and how it could be done better. This extensively revised edition includes developments such as the Work Profiling System and the competency framework.

1993   144 pages   ISBN 0 85292 542 5   **£15.95**

Negotiation Skills and Strategies
Alan Fowler

Second edition

This excellent introductory text shows managers how to negotiate for positive results. It offers concrete practical guidance on everything from setting objectives and agendas through to agreement and implementation, as well as bargaining by correspondence and effective use of media. Lively case-studies and check-lists drive home the key messages.

1996   160 pages   ISBN 0 85292 664 2   **£14.95**

Training Needs Analysis and Evaluation
Frances and Roland Bee

Training needs must be driven from business needs and a corporate strategy developed in response to internal and external stimuli. Once the need has been clearly specified, all the more technical issues fall easily into place. The evaluation process then allows managers to assess whether training has been successful.

1994   320 pages   ISBN 0 85292 547 6   **£16.95**

Assessment Centres
Charles Woodruffe

Second edition

This acclaimed book explains how assessment centres, when tailored to the specific needs of individual organisations, can be a crucial tool for selection and development. The author examines design and delivery; personnel and participants; feedback and training; and validation techniques.

1994   240 pages   ISBN 0 85292 545 X   **£17.95**

Employee Induction: A good start
Alan Fowler

Third edition

This well-established text has been fully revised to take account of the latest legislation and the issues raised by today's far more diverse and flexible workforce.

1996   104 pages   ISBN 0 85292 645 6   **£10.95**

Recruitment Advertising: Right first time
John Courtis

The ideal recruiter's companion, this book shows how, by following a few simple principles, managers can choose appropriate and
cost-effective media and make the most efficient use of advertising space.

1994   104 pages   ISBN 0 85292 558 1   **£10.95**